Merseyside's Old Firm?
The Sectarian Roots of Everton and Liverpool Football Clubs.

By David Kennedy

Acknowledgements

I am indebted in particular to Dr Peter Kennedy and Mr John Campbell for their advice concerning this work. Their expertise on the identity politics of Merseyside football and the social significance of football more generally was invaluable to me in the construction of this volume. I would also like to thank my family for their consideration and support throughout, and I dedicate this book to them.

Without the expertise of the staff at the following institutions the archival material required to complete my book would have been much more difficult — if not impossible — to unearth, and I offer them my gratitude to them: The British Newspaper Library, Collindale, London; Brotherton Library, University of Leeds; Companies House, Cardiff; Grand Lodge Library, London; Harold Cohen and Sydney Jones Library, University of Liverpool; Liverpool Public Record Office; Liverpool Probate District registry; Public Record Office, Kew; Probate Department, Principal Registry of the Family Division, High Holborn. I thank also the following individuals who provided particular guidance on certain archival sources and access to them: Mike Braham, Secretary of Southport Liberal Association; Geoff Brandwood, Chair of Liverpool West Derby Conservative Association; Rebecca Coombes, The Library and

Museum of Freemasonry, Freemason's Hall, London; Lee Le Clerque, Secretary of the North West Brewers' and Licensed Retailers Association.

Preface

Most football supporters are aware of the deep divisions in Glasgow football between Celtic and Rangers – divisions rooted in the age old religious and political conflicts of the west of Scotland. That complex rivalry is collapsed into the catchall term "Old Firm" to denote the mutually reinforcing (and financially beneficial) nature of the relationship of those football clubs. Previously the impact of religion and ethnicity on football in mainland Britain has been discussed in terms of its contribution to the cultural development of Scotland – with the rivalry of Edinburgh's Heart of Midlothian and Hibernian football clubs also the subject of similar (if less intense) examination. This volume, though, turns its attention south of the border to address that age-old question of whether sectarian affiliations can be attached to the Merseyside giants: Everton and Liverpool football clubs. Does the term "Old Firm" have any sort of resonance with the two great clubs of this once sectarian blighted city?

There is a prodigious amount of anecdotal evidence claiming Everton to be the team traditionally supported by the city's Catholic population and Liverpool predominantly supported by Protestants — a proposition summarily dismissed by most commentators as more urban myth than reality. The issue, though, has never been investigated in any great depth and deserves closer scrutiny than the cursory attention it has hitherto been afforded by researchers. There remains an enduring fascination with this somewhat controversial subject. What has been absent from the debate, however, is a dispassionate quest for knowledge about the claimed division backed up by authentic and detailed research. The idea of this book is to provide this by adding documentary evidence to the anecdotal evidence that the subject has trundled along on for decades.

The objective here isn't to pin the present day Everton and Liverpool football clubs to a particular heritage but to establish a more substantial basis upon which an informed conclusion of the claimed historical Everton-Catholic/Liverpool-Protestant division can be made.

Dr David Kennedy 2017

Cover portraits: George Mahon, Everton FC first chairman; John Houlding, Liverpool FC first chairman

Table of Contents

Introduction

Sectarianism in the City of Liverpool

Politicians in Control of Everton and Liverpool Football Clubs

Masonic Influence in the Boardroom of Liverpool FC

Identification with Different Ethnic and Religious Groups at Everton and Liverpool Football Clubs?

Conclusion

Appendices

Bibliography

Introduction

> People 'dressed' their houses to advertise Cup Final footballing allegiances, though my Mum would never allow my brother's Evertonian blue to go up in case neighbours or passers-by mistakenly took us for Catholics – John Williams (football sociologist).[1]
>
> It was strange in the 1930s for a Catholic to support Liverpool – John Woods (Liverpool author).[2]
>
> In Liverpool, even in the two-ups and two-downs, most Protestants were Conservative and most Catholics were Labour, just as Everton was the Catholic team and Liverpool the Proddy-Dog one – Cilla Black (singer).[3]
>
> Being a Roman Catholic school, religion played a large part in our school life. Pop Moran even tried to turn me off football at Anfield – Catholics were traditionally Everton supporters and players; Liverpool were the Protestant team. Pop honestly thought that being a Catholic I wouldn't be happy at Anfield – Tommy Smith (ex Liverpool FC player and captain).[4]

A sectarian division between Everton and Liverpool football clubs is, for some, an irrefutable part of local football culture. There is a prodigious amount of anecdotal evidence claiming Everton to be the team traditionally supported by the city's Catholic population and Liverpool being predominantly supported by Protestants.[5] For others, however, sectarian affiliation is more urban myth than reality: a tribal impulse amongst some fans to shore up and sharpen their own identity by suggesting a deeper meaning to support for the two clubs. Orthodox opinion lies with the latter viewpoint and football historians in particular have dismissed notions of sectarianism as having no foundation, declaring it an unwanted and divisive intrusion into the study of both clubs. The issue, though, has never been investigated in any great depth and it deserves closer scrutiny than the cursory attention afforded it. This is a point made by Glasgow football historian and author of the book *The Old Firm* – a social history of Glasgow Rangers and Glasgow Celtic. Murray correctly states that 'There is a strange silence surrounding the religious associations of the two big Liverpool clubs. For a city [Liverpool] to be so profoundly affected by sectarianism in all areas of civil life to apparently leave no mark on football beggars belief; the lack of analysis given to the subject a serious omission'.[6] Whilst the claim of religious differences has little or no meaning in defining the relationship of the modern day Everton and Liverpool football clubs, the specific question to address is whether there is any justification for the perception that, in an earlier period, the basis for such claims *did* exist?

Naturally, claims of past sectarian connections have been resisted strongly by both clubs. Official club literature goes to some lengths to deny the possibility. Everton and Liverpool football club official histories stress shared origins in the Methodist chapel school, St Domingo - said to have played a foundational role in Merseyside football - and downplay what they view as baseless claims of Catholic/Protestant sectarian divisions. However, it would be a mistake to dismiss the claims that each club has acted as standard-bearer for distinct communities simply because of their shared point of origin. In fact, this claimed point of origin looks to be somewhat exaggerated.

There is surprisingly little evidence relating to the St Domingo chapel football team and the chapel's surviving records make no reference to its setting up one. Our only knowledge of its influence comes from the writings of men like William C. Cuff, a director and chairman of Everton whose family had been congregants of the St Domingo chapel, and from Thomas Keates the club's first historian and an early director of Everton FC. Both men emphasize the role played by the chapel side (established in 1878) in the club's formation. A possible motive for this presentation of chapel origins, and certainly with regard to Cuff, was the view that football was a force for moral good. This was something he continually stressed in his zealous opposition to the encroachment of commercial associations with football in later years, particularly through gambling and alcohol. However, in their accounts both men also mention the debt the nascent Everton owed to players from other churches in the district. With this ecumenical coalescing of football talent, the adoption of the name 'Everton' was an obvious choice and this took place at the end of 1879. From all of this it is perhaps a little creative to suggest a single definitive source for Everton FC. Instead it points toward a number of tributaries. Indeed, whatever the original influence church and chapel football teams may have had on the club's formation these (tenuous) links were quickly superseded. The newly formed Everton FC became more solidly associated with public houses. Initially the club's headquarters were at the Queen's Head Inn, Everton, and then at brewer and club president Councilor John Houlding's Sandon Hotel, Anfield.

Notwithstanding the establishment of Everton as a leading English top flight club in the 1880s (culminating in 1891/92 with their first English title), the real beginning of the Merseyside football story in any substantial sense was when the factional split within the committee of Everton FC brought Liverpool FC into existence in 1892 – a tumultuous moment that shaped the region's, and indeed the nation's, football destiny.

Partly the result of a financial dispute between president John Houlding and club committee members, but with obvious political overtones, the split of 1892 sees the emergence onto the football scene of a body of men with strong political identities. The local newspaper, *The Liverpool Echo* – surveying the period of the Everton split three decades after it happened – captured the divisions thus:

> Although himself [John Houlding] a strong party politician for the Tories and with an utter detestation of everything savouring of Liberalism or Radicalism, he strangely enough had amongst his warmest football supporters keen young Liberals and sturdy teetotal Nonconformists, who held equally as strong political and social views. Yet both he and they kept their views in sturdy independence of each other, and on the common ground of Everton Football Club. The great Tory dictator of Everton and the young Liberal and Radical clubmen met together weekly in warm and earnest mutual endeavor. But alas! That state of affairs did not continue or we should not today have both Everton and Liverpool clubs.
> (Liverpool Echo: April 25th 1925)

§

The men who controlled the fortunes of Everton and Liverpool football clubs, then, also took an active part in local politics.

In the years before its split the club experienced deep and bitter factionalism at committee level – factionalism steeped in personal rivalries and shot-through with political agendas. As per Murray's comment above, it would be strange given the particular political environment in the City of Liverpool during this period had this football conflict remained untouched from matters of religious controversy and discretely contained in a purely sporting context. To understand why this would be the case it is necessary to take a short detour into the sectarian history of Liverpool politics.

Sectarianism in the City of Liverpool

During the pioneering period of professional football in Liverpool religious sectarianism dominated civic affairs and impacted on everyday life: housing, schooling, the provision of welfare and the city's occupational structure were all tribally contested territory. The source for this was the massive influx of Irish immigration into the city in the second half of the nineteenth century and the host community's reception for them. By the mid-nineteenth century almost a quarter of the city's population were Irish-born, as Liverpool became a key destination point for an exodus of Irish Protestants and Catholics seeking to escape the ravages of famine and economic downturn. Friction between the city's Protestant and Catholic populations was a feature of the social landscape – on many occasions erupting into street violence and rioting between ethnically divided communities. Some historians have argued that the ferocity of the hostility between Irish Catholics in Liverpool and the "native" British Protestant and Irish Protestant community surpassed the sectarian divide in the west of Scotland and only stands close comparison with the experience of towns in Northern Ireland: 'Liverpool – sister of Belfast, rough, big hearted, Protestant and Unionist'.[7]

Liverpool has long had the reputation of being an "Irish city". It would during the period stretching between mid-nineteenth century and mid-twentieth century, however, be more accurate to describe Liverpool as an Orange city.

The Loyal Orange Institution (more commonly known as the Orange Order) is a Protestant fraternal body with its roots in eighteenth century Ireland. It is sworn to maintain the union between Britain and Ireland and Protestant ascendancy over Roman Catholics in the United Kingdom. Traditionally its heartland has traditionally been the north of Ireland, but in the nineteenth century the organization had a huge influence on everyday life in parts of mainland Britain, particularly in towns and cities where there was a large influx of Irish immigrants. Liverpool became the major port of entry and settlement for the Irish diaspora in England, and subsequently became the base for the largest and most active Orange Order in the country. Organizationally, Liverpool Orangeism was at its height in the late nineteenth century and early twentieth century with a membership of over 30,000 who were serviced by almost two hundred lodges in the Liverpool Province. This period was also the height of its political influence when it held sway over the fortunes of Liverpool Conservatism.

Certainly, the best way to boost the prospects of a political party or candidate in Liverpool at this time would have been to embrace Orange convictions. At election times the sheer number of Orange Order members could be deployed in order to make or break political campaigns. As the mainstream party viewed by many as the political representation of the ties between Church and state, the Tories enjoyed a fruitful relationship with the Orange Order and, through them, the Protestant majority amongst the electorate. Liverpool's Tory Party hierarchy traditionally played on the emotions of the Protestant working class of the city by appealing beyond their class interests to their religious identity. This brand of popular Toryism carried the day in Liverpool. Deference shown to the Tory elite by the Protestant working class (and their support at the ballot box) was rewarded by the party's close identification with the values and institutions the Protestant working class held in esteem – above all, the Orange Order. It also guaranteed their implacable opposition to any significant improvement in the condition of the Irish Catholic working class, more especially in the fiercely competitive casual labour market of dockland Liverpool. By expertly playing the Orange card in this way the Tories retained municipal control of Liverpool well into the twentieth century.

The zenith of the Order's sway over Liverpool Conservatism was marked in 1912 on the occasion of the huge demonstration of support for Sir Edward Carson's visit to Liverpool in his efforts to oppose Home Rule for Ireland. A quarter of a million people turned out to a demonstration held at the city's Shiel Park. In attendance was Archibald Salvidge, the leader of the Liverpool Conservative Party, himself the political product of sectarian based organisations. Salvidge welcomed Carson, stating he wanted to be there to 'shake [Carson] by the hand'. It was one of the most important gatherings of Unionism ever assembled on the British mainland and it had been orchestrated by the Liverpool Conservative and Unionist Party.

'The successful penetration of Liverpool's political culture by a strong Orange tendency' state historians, Belchem and MacRaild, 'was unmatched anywhere in Britain. Orangeism became part of Liverpool's civic culture in ways that even Glasgow did not match'.[8] In Liverpool, then, xenophobia and religious sectarianism gained legitimacy and became, in Tory hands, the chosen tools to secure civic power. The city's Conservative Party fueled prejudice toward the Irish and toward second and third generation Irish, spreading fear amongst the native British Protestant population about economic rivalry and their ruination at the hands of the "invaders".

But politics in Liverpool was coloured by an Orange *and* Green palette. Unlike their political adversaries, though, the politics of the Liverpool Irish was not primarily focused upon the town in which they lived but on their homeland (or the homeland of their fathers and grandfathers). The Liverpool Scotland constituency in the heart of "Irish Liverpool", for example, elected an Irish Nationalist MP, Thomas Powers O'Connor to Westminster. This was the only constituency outside of Ireland ever to return an Irish Nationalist MP. O'Connor kept his seat between 1889 and his death in 1929 – unopposed from 1918 onward - such was the strength of nationalist feeling in this part of the city. Though an Irish electoral machine in the Scotland and Vauxhall council wards where there was a concentration of Liverpool Irish would eventually broaden its objectives out to matters of a more municipal nature by the early part of the twentieth century (addressing the everyday material issues their electoral base struggled with), Irish politics in the city was firmly fixed on imperial affairs.

On these matters the Irish in Liverpool had a long association and alliance with the city's Liberal Party. The Liberals despised the sectarian politics of Orangeism and supported reforms aimed at gaining social equality for Catholics. The pact that existed between the Liverpool Irish and the Liverpool Liberal Party was based on this common ground and cemented by their mutual objective of securing Irish Home Rule. This paved the way for a local electoral deal between the two forces. The "deal" was a largely informal arrangement whereby Irish Nationalist League candidates would often be stood down in council wards where Liberal candidates had a better chance of carrying the day against Conservative Party candidates, and vice versa. By forging an alliance with the local Irish party, therefore, the Liberal Party tended to be seen in most people's eyes as a political force that defended the rights of Catholics in the city. Their political rivals predictably put the matter more bluntly. Liverpool's Tory leader William B. Forwood offered to the municipal electorate in 1892 the stark choice of being either:

> ...well governed by the Conservative Party as it had for the past 50 years, or governed by Home Rulers who had no interest whatever in Liverpool but were simply in the city council to further the political interests of Home Rule in Ireland. It was not a question of handing over the control of the council to Messrs Holt, Bowring and Rathbone [Liberal Party grandees] but to Messrs Lynskey, Taggart and Kelly [Irish Nationalist councillors].[9]

Politics in the city, therefore, became synonymous with ethno-religious conflict, as a Liberal-Nationalist bloc faced off against a Tory-Orange caucus.

Liverpool was a harsh environment for the class-based politics found elsewhere in England at this time to prosper in. The local Labour Party struggled to gain the attention of the working class electorate until the second half of the twentieth century. 'Liverpool', the frustrated Labour Party leader Ramsey MacDonald wrote in 1910, 'is rotten and we better recognise it'.[10] Such was the ethno-religious cleavage amongst the electorate in Liverpool it would be well into the twentieth century before the Labour Party in the city became a significant electoral force – an event usually attributed to the disintegration of separate Irish representation and the mutation of Irish politics into the politics of the Labour Party. Prior to this, the local Home Rule supporting Liberal Party and the Conservative-Unionist Party were much more adept than the Labour Movement at competing for civic power by appealing to ethno-religious prejudices and divisions.

§

The important take away message from all of this is that, whereas in other towns during this period the issues primarily to be addressed and contested by the major parties in local politics would be the more prosaic matters of, say, housing and health provision, the setting of rates, or the employment rights of municipal workers, in Liverpool "Imperial affairs" (that is, religion and the Irish Question) were paramount. The city was split asunder by competing rival identities which dominated the local political scene and reached into its social and cultural life: Irish versus British; Nationalist versus Unionist; immigrant versus native. For this reason, it would be completely understandable for many ordinary

Liverpudlians to attach ethno-religious labels to Everton and Liverpool football clubs if there was seen to be a high incidence of their most visible representatives active in local Liberal and Conservative parties *and* who were opposed to each other in significant number across the football divide. With this possibility in mind, the political-sectarian associations of both clubs' hierarchies will be explored in the next chapter.

Politicians in Control of Everton and Liverpool Football Clubs

The factional divisions in the old Everton club were resolved after the split of 1892 with a reconstituted Everton FC and the creation of a newly established Liverpool FC. With control over their respective clubs, both bodies of men who opposed each other in the old Everton Committee had the freedom to manoeuvre and pursue their preferred strategy of organisational growth without restraint. This was reflected in the dramatically different styles of governance adopted: especially concerning the democratic rights of members to have a say in the running of their club and over directors' commercial rights as vendors.

At Everton, ownership was dispersed amongst a large number of shareholders holding small amounts of stock; whereas at Liverpool FC ownership was concentrated in the hands of a few club directors. The new board at Everton sought to retain the old organisation's identity as a member's club into the limited company era by fulfilling their promise to keep the base of financial control of the club as wide as possible. Significantly, given the furore in the original club over its financial exploitation, the proportion of share ownership amongst directors remained low at Everton. The establishment of a system of one member-one vote at the club reinforced membership control.

If a consideration of the rights of the ordinary shareholder and supporter can be said to have accompanied Everton's transition to limited company status, the creation of Liverpool FC as a limited company provides us with evidence of a somewhat different agenda. Once the obstacles placed in the path of the commercial designs of Houlding and his allies had been removed the commercial rights of the board, and the concentration of power therein, were immediately established at Liverpool FC. A motion carried at the club's first Annual General Meeting in 1892 is instructive as to the impulse of those setting-up the club: 'The office of director shall not be vacated by his being concerned or participating in the profits of supplying the company with any goods or stock, or otherwise contracting with the company or for execution of any work for the company'.[11]

If the split of 1892 put into practice opposing corporate visions vying with each other for supremacy in the old club, the establishment of two separate clubs disentangled the manifest political divisions within it too. In the years following the Split of 1892 the Everton boardroom became a stronghold of men involved in Liberal politics. Conversely, the Liverpool boardroom was the almost exclusive preserve of men involved in Conservative politics.

In the Everton boardroom, surgeon Dr James Clement Baxter was Liberal city councilor for St. Anne's ward. Baxter was a devout Roman Catholic whose services to the poor and infirm of his parish, St Francis Xaviers in Everton, were commemorated in a stained glass window erected in his honour at that church. His family wealth – made through theatre ownership - allowed him to put forward the bulk of the £2,000 Everton required to begin work on their new home at Goodison Park. The football club became something of a family concern with Baxter's son, Cecil (another Liberal councillor) later following him into the boardroom at Everton. Dublin-born George Mahon, Everton's first chairman, was a committee member of Walton Liberal Association. Mahon, an accountant by profession, was something of a polymath – lecturing in microscopic and astronomical studies around the City.[12] Fellow Irishman, Dr William Whitford, joined Mahon on the board of directors. Whitford was chairman of Everton and Kirkdale Liberal Association. He was also an outspoken figure against the drink trade – a man the *Liverpool Review* dubbed 'the elect hero of the fire and sword teetotallers'. This temperance zeal was something he shared with Everton and Liberal Party colleague, William Robert Clayton. Clayton, a bookkeeper, was the chairman of Formby Liberal Association and gave lectures to temperance groups including the

Formby Congregational School's Band of Hope. Yet another Everton director holding political office was Alfred Gates: the leader of the Liberal Party in Liverpool City Council. And three more Everton directors: Will Cuff (a future President of the Football League), Benjamin Kelly and Arthur Riley Wade, though not holding formal office, were involved in Liberal politics in the city; all being frequently mentioned in local press reports covering ward level meetings in the north end of Liverpool. All but one of the nine men mentioned above would become chairmen of Everton prior to the Second World War.[13]

These men also attracted support for the club from influential Liberal figures outside of it. Financial aid to break the club free from its Anfield home - and therefore its reliance on John Houlding - came from two industrialists: William Pickles Hartley, the fruit preserve manufacturer, and Robert William Hudson, the son and heir of soap manufacturer Robert Spiers Hudson. Hartley was a 'staunch Liberal' in politics, representing the Liberal Party in the city council chamber; Hudson was Everton director Dr Whitford's predecessor as chairman of the Kirkdale Liberal Association. Finances were also forthcoming from Irishman Dr John Elliott Dimond, a friend and Liberal Party associate of Dr James Clement Baxter. In point of fact, and as can probably be discerned, there was a strong Irish contingent amongst the early post-split Everton boardroom. Besides Mahon and Whitford another Irishman, customs officer Abraham Thomas Coates, was voted in as a director of the club in 1892. James Clement Baxter was second generation Irish and, like Dr William Whitford, trained to become a surgeon in Ireland.[14]

By contrast, the politics of the men at the helm of Liverpool FC was of a distinctly Conservative nature. Seven directors: Benjamin E. Bailey, Edwin Berry, John Houlding, William Houlding, Ephraim Walker, John McKenna, Laurence Crosthwaite and one club secretary, Simon Jude, were members of the Constitutional Association (the ruling body of Liverpool Conservatism). The Constitutional Association exercised complete control over district Conservative Associations in Liverpool and its affiliated societies and organizations, such as the Loyal Orange Institution. In the council chamber, directors John Houlding, Edwin Berry, Ephraim Walker, William Houlding (John Houlding's son and fellow director), and club secretary Simon Jude were Conservative councilors representing north Liverpool wards. Other Liverpool FC directors involved in Conservative politics were Harry Oldfield Cooper, a member of the Liverpool Junior Conservative Club, Thomas Croft Howarth, a figure key in the formation of the club and the leader of the Conservative group in the Liverpool Parliamentary Debating Society, and Thomas Ashmole, a Conservative and Unionist Alderman on Wallasey Borough Council. [15]

As with the group of men in control of Everton, the men who set up Liverpool FC enjoyed the support of senior political figures within the city. James A Willox, the proprietor of the local Conservative-leaning newspaper, the *Liverpool Courier* and the Conservative MP for Everton, swung his paper's editorial weight behind the newly created Liverpool FC and also bought shares in the club. Willox placed one of his employees, John Dermot, to sit on the Liverpool board as a proxy. Another "big beast" of the local political scene onside with the men from Anfield was Belfast-born Thomas McCracken, the Deputy Grandmaster of the Orange Order (Liverpool Province). He was a man who waged war with the local Conservative organization in the north end of Liverpool and within the district of Everton in particular over what he perceived to be a "softening" approach from official Conservative candidates concerning their stance on religious affairs – that is, their failure to espouse staunch enough Protestant politics for the working men of the district to rally around in the face of the growing electoral challenge from what he saw as a caucus of Roman Catholics, Liberals and "Radicals". McCracken became a close associate with the board of directors at Liverpool FC in the club's early period, even to the extent of joining that body for a short period in the mid-1890s. Houlding and McCracken appear to be particularly connected; friends as well as politically singing from the same hymn sheet, the two men traveled abroad together on drink trade business. McCracken was a man Houlding described as 'a decades old friend'. Their involvement together at Liverpool FC – along with other longstanding Orange allies of Houlding - Joseph Williams and James Freeman Booth - is highly significant and, as we shall see, indicates the club hierarchy to have been firmly at the forefront of a hard line struggle against the immigrant Catholic Irish in Liverpool.[16]

From this comparison we can see how polarized the two groups of leaders of the city's premier football clubs were in matters of civic politics – an opposition that often boiled over into personal enmity, particularly between the two acknowledged leaders of the clubs in the early years of their rivalry: George Mahon of Everton and John Houlding of Liverpool. Mahon and Houlding were men who crossed swords with each other at the ballot and in the local press on a number of occasions, and a long-standing political grudge festered between them, both before and after the 1892 split. Mahon was the Liberal candidate in the Walton Local Board elections of 1887 in which Houlding acted as election agent to Mahon's opponent, Tory Councillor Dr John Utting. Mahon narrowly defeated Utting in a stormy contest that Houlding did much to whip up.[17] On another occasion in 1889, Mahon, in his capacity as returning officer for the Walton Division of Lancashire County Council, incensed Houlding, who was acting as the election agent for Tory candidate (and fellow brewer) Sir David Radcliffe seeking office in that authority, by rejecting Radcliffe's nomination on a technicality. Houlding accused Mahon of political sabotage, further complaining that bill posters bearing Mahon's name 'had been used to cover a large number of posters announcing Conservative Party meetings' in the district of Walton.[18] The Intense dislike for each other and their opposing political views was widely known, prompting the *Liverpool Echo* to suggest in the aftermath of the hostile split of the old Everton club that Mahon should come out and directly challenge Houlding for his Everton and Kirkdale ward seat in the upcoming local elections.[19]

It is difficult to believe that such a stark contrast in the political complexion of those serving on Everton and Liverpool's board of directors and the caliber of the men supporting them would have escaped the attention of a local population keenly tuned-in to the attitudes of those in public life on matters of religion, politics and particularly Irish affairs. In fact, there were many public statements made by prominent club representatives of both Everton and Liverpool football clubs concerning the issues of religion, ethnicity and the all-pervasive matter of Irish Home Rule – statements which would have driven home their differences for any interested outside audience. For example, Everton director Dr William Whitford - described in the local press as 'an ardent Home-Ruler' - made an impassioned speech during the municipal election campaign of 1892 against the blocking of Irish Home Rule by Ulster Unionists:

> Ulstermen do not desire to govern Ireland according to the wishes of the people of Ireland, but according to the narrow prejudices of the so-called "loyal minority". Irish Catholic bishops and priests had not the illegitimate power we in this country are asked to believe. Their views are, however, in accordance with the nationalist aspirations of the Irish people. The priests had been loyal to the people, unlike the priests of other denominations...The Irish priests could not and had not the power to lead the Irish people in temporal matters against their honest convictions.[20]

Another Everton director, Liberal councilor Alfred Gates (a name which was 'as a red rag to a furious bull' to the Conservative-Unionist Party, according to the *Liverpool Daily Post*), was a 'strenuous advocate of Home Rule' and keen to show that 'the Orange Tory Party were losing ground in Liverpool'. Speaking to a Liberal-Nationalist audience, Gates suggested that 'if Liberalism had a little of the enthusiasm and spirit of the Irish it would be in a better position today'.[21] For his part, George Mahon reorganised Walton Liberal Association in the wake of the defection of Liberal Unionists who were opposed to Liberal national leader Liverpool-born William Ewart Gladstone's stance on the Irish Question. Mahon was a prime mover in the Walton Liberal Party's adoption of the plank of Irish Home Rule and their stated task toward helping secure this end was to 'do all we can to establish the Liberal Party in the council...we will never get Liberal representatives to parliament until we destroy the power of the Conservatives in the city council'.[22]

From figures amongst the Liverpool FC hierarchy, on the other hand, there was an equally strident and public outpouring of feeling toward the Protestant-Unionist cause. Founder and Chairman of Liverpool FC, John Houlding, quite obviously found it difficult to contain his religious leanings as a Conservative-Unionist and an Orangeman whilst carrying out his duties as a Guardian at the West Derby Poor Law Union. Guardian's were elected to their positions by rate payers and were responsible for the administration of poor relief in their area – in this instance a huge swathe of land that encompassed the whole of the north end districts of Liverpool and beyond to neighbouring towns, such as Bootle, Seaforth, Waterloo and Crosby making it the biggest Poor Law Union in the country. Houlding held huge power and he pointedly refused granting to Catholic priests any payment for ministering to Catholic inmates of workhouses within his jurisdiction whilst allowing such payment to Church of England and Nonconformist ministers. In a letter published in the *Liverpool Courier,* Houlding set out his opposition to a motion put before the Poor Law Union to also allow payment to Catholic priests as an act of justice and common fairness:

> I defy any member of the Board or any judge in the land to show me an Act of Parliament which expressly stated that they should pay Roman Catholics for services performed in workhouses. If English Unions did appoint a Roman Catholic priest it is only done by a clear evasion of the law, and often perhaps for the sake of quietness.[23]

Another Liverpool FC director, Edwin Berry, the successor to John Houlding as club chairman, made plain his opposition to the re-emergence of an influential Roman Catholic Church in British society. Addressing an audience of the National Protestant Union in 1898, an Evangelical Anglican body committed to helping "sound Protestant" candidates at elections, Berry offered his support to 'the repression of lawlessness and Romanising influence', declaring himself to be a 'loyal Churchman with every desire to further the principles of the Church of England in accordance with the Reformation'. This was a position he reiterated six years later when, attempting to outflank the challenge of an independent Orange Order candidate for his Liverpool council seat, Berry described himself as being 'zealous to bring Ritualistic offenders to book'.[24] The aforementioned MP for Everton, James A Willox, was President of the National Protestant Union. The proprietor of the *Liverpool Courier* was a religious firebrand, more particularly in defence of British dominion over Ireland. Willox, speaking to a meeting in his parliamentary constituency, attacked Liberal policy on Ireland thus: 'To conciliate four million people in Ireland are we going to sacrifice one million and a half of loyal Protestants and faithful lieges of the

Queen?'. To another Conservative audience Willox called for 'more of Cromwell's courage and more of his religion in public life'.[25]

Crucially, the Unionist credentials of Liverpool FCs hierarchy are firmly underlined by the connections many of its directors had with a body called the Liverpool Working Men's Conservative Association (WMCA), an organisation affiliated to the Tory Party. The overlap of personnel between the football club and this avowedly Protestant organisation gives us further scope to understand how perceptions of a sectarian football division between Everton and Liverpool could have gained traction at this historical juncture.

Described by Barbara Whittingham-Jones, a local political journalist, as 'the engine of Protestant power' within Liverpool Conservatism, the WMCA were at the vanguard of anti-Catholic politics in the City of Liverpool. To gain an appreciation of the nature of this organization we can turn to the words of Whittingham-Jones written at the height of the WMCA's power in the Inter War period. She describes here the proceedings on her visit to one branch meeting in 1936:

> Meetings at Conservative clubs cannot proceed until an incantation has first been declared by all present. The chairman opens the meeting by requiring members who have been guilty of 'consorting' with Catholics to confess their delinquencies and upon doing so they then receive a warning. Catholics who have

> strayed in by chance are requested to leave the room. Even Questions have to be preceded by the formula: "By my Protestant faith and Conservative principles..." with hand raised in the Hitler salute. Such is the democratic character of this sectarian class-ridden caucus that no Roman Catholic workingmen can join the Conservative Party in Liverpool or frequent the Workingmen's Conservative Association clubs.[26]

The WMCA and the Orange Order in Liverpool, Whittingham-Jones goes on to state, were as 'identical in political outlook as in personnel [an organization] held together by its tough Orange fibre'.

The Liverpool WMCA was predictably staunch on the Irish Question, offering its unwavering support for the maintenance of the Union with Ireland. The Association's policy prior to the partition of Ireland was to oppose the breaking up of the Union and to back the reprisals carried out by the British auxiliary force: the notoriously brutal Black and Tans, against Irish Republicans. Writing in 1920, the Liverpool WMCA Chairman, Sir Archibald Salvidge, saluted Black and Tan operations as the actions of '...those who will not submit meekly to the fiendish destruction of life and property which Sinn Fein gunmen claim as noble acts of heroism [but, rather] give Sinn Feiners a taste of their own medicine'. In the aftermath of the setting up of the Irish Free State in 1921, the Liverpool organisation's emphasis merely switched to the safeguarding of Protestant Ulster and the adoption (no doubt with one eye on local affairs) of "No Surrender" Unionist politics.[27]

35

The amount of people involved in the ownership and control of Liverpool FC who were also key figures in the WMCA is quite remarkable and telling. They included such club luminaries as John Houlding, Edwin Berry and Benjamin Bailey – all chairmen of Liverpool FC prior to the First World War and key figures in this quasi-religious organisation. Another club director, Ephraim P. Walker, described by the *Liverpool Daily Post* as a "staunch and faithful Churchman", was a member of the WMCA's governing council. The earlier mentioned Thomas McCracken was chairman of the Low Hill WMCA. And at shareholder level too the connection was significant. John Holland, one of the small number of shareholders of Liverpool FC when it was formed in 1892 and who remained a shareholder until his death in 1914 was a founding member of the Liverpool WMCA and its longstanding secretary, and James A. Willox was Vice President of this organisation. Yet another significant Liverpool FC shareholding connection with the WMCA was that of Bents Brewery. Bents held shares in Liverpool FC at a time when control of the brewery was in the hands of Archibald Salvidge, Chairman of the WMCA and Edward J. Chevalier, Vice Chairman of the organization. And the Liverpool FC link with this sectarian body proved to be a longstanding affair, stretching beyond the First World War to the 1930s and 1940s. Club director Albert Edward Berry succeeded his brother Edwin as WMCA solicitor in 1925, holding the position until 1931. This post was then passed on to yet another Liverpool FC director and Conservative councilor, Ralph Knowles Milne, a position he held until his death in 1954. The club's sometime solicitor and secretary in the 1940s, Maxwell Fyffe, the Conservative MP for Liverpool West Derby constituency, also maintained the connection between Liverpool FC and the WMCA when he, in turn, took over solicitor duties from Milne.

Indeed, these ties between leading lights of the club and the WMCA were of practical assistance. Houlding's difficulties in retaining his council seat in 1891 – something he and the *Liverpool Courier* were placing at the door of "Radicals" within the Everton FC committee – prompted the Kirkdale branch of this sectarian organization to publicly back Houlding and condemn those at Everton FC seeking to use football 'as a lever in their efforts towards his defeat'. At this same point, John McCracken chaired a meeting of the Orange Order called to offer its support to Houlding. Orange Order endorsements were something Houlding had enjoyed before in his political life. At a Battle of the Boyne celebration on July 12th 1885, Houlding - seeking the support of the Orange Order for his Everton and Kirkdale ward candidature - was paraded along with another Tory-Orange candidate, Councillor Thomas Bland Royden (a future MP for Toxteth and a man known by the soubriquet "Protestant Tommy of Toxteth"). A speaker at the event told his audience: 'Orangemen were duty-bound to work tooth and nail, heart and soul, to return them top of the poll. [Houlding and Royden] had never forsaken the Orange body in the past and Orangemen would not forsake them now. The uncompromising support which both candidates had always given to Protestantism and Conservatism warranted them in relying on the support of every member of the Orange body.'[28]

§

So what does this information tell us about the men taking their place in Liverpool FCs hierarchy? One thing it tells us is that their fierce strain of anti-Catholicism - in words and deeds - were consistent with (and played upon) popular British Protestant fears of being "over-run" by Irish Catholic immigration: a familiar riff in Liverpool politics, but one at its loudest at the end of the nineteenth century and early twentieth century. It also tells us that these men held prominent positions within sectarian organisations in the City of Liverpool such as the Working Men's Conservative Association and the Orange Order and presented themselves to the Protestant working class as champions of a British identity – bulwarks against "Popery" and the degradation of living standards they argued it represented in the form of an influx of Irish Catholics competing for employment in the port city's economy. Protestantism was their unifying bond and Catholicism was viewed as the alien belief of an alien people: the Liverpool Irish. Consistent with the organisations they were members of, they did not view either Irish immigrants or their offspring as *bona fide* citizens of Liverpool. The dual identity of second and third generation Irish Catholics as being both British *and* Irish was not to be recognized. They afforded no space to Catholics to establish a significant presence in "respectable" Liverpool society. If that space became a possibility it would be opposed and closed down – as we witnessed above in Liverpool FC owner John Houlding's statement regarding the equal treatment of Roman Catholic clergy in attendance of their co-religionists passing through his West Derby Poor Law Union fiefdom.

Yet as we saw, and as much as the attacks and harrying of Irish Catholics was the stamp of Protestant Unionists like Houlding and his fellow football club directors, much of their vitriol was aimed at English (Protestant) religious and political figures deemed to be "soft' on Roman Catholics – that is, too close to that religion for their liking, and too sympathetic to the plight of the Irish. We have seen how men from the Liverpool FC hierarchy such as Edwin Berry and James A. Willox were involved in organisations committed to a purist version of Protestantism and who spoke passionately about the dangerous advance of "Ritualism" within the Church of England (the adoption of the trappings and ceremony of

Roman Catholic mass). Their antipathy toward Gladstonian Liberalism was driven by their Protestant Unionist insistence that support for Home Rule meant the acceptance of "Rome Rule" in Britain. In the Tory rhetoric of the day their opponents: the Gladstonian Liberals were "Disloyalists" - men treacherous to British values and probably the Empire itself.

These are important contextual points to bear in mind when considering the undoubtedly hostile relations between the Liverpool and Everton boardrooms of the period. The bad blood that flowed between these men was already present after the bruising conflict that accompanied the split of Everton FC in 1892. We can be sure that the staunch Unionists in the Liverpool boardroom would have taken a very dim view indeed of their counterparts from across Stanley Park for offering succor to that part of the city's population they regarded as the enemy within – the Catholic Irish; the support of a core of men in the Everton boardroom for Home Rule would have been seen as an unforgivable act of treachery. For an institution as famous locally and nationally (and as culturally important as Everton FC) to come within the orbit and sway of men with Irish sympathies (and, worse still, Irish Nationalist sympathies) would have been viewed as both alarming and repugnant, and an open declaration of war.

With respect to football clubs and their close associations with Protestant Unionist organisations, it is interesting to note that the Glasgow Working Men's' Conservative Association were equally central to the early development of Glasgow Rangers FC.[29] The reputation of the Glasgow club as a bulwark of Protestant and Unionist ascendancy in the West of Scotland is well established. The undoubted influence of the Liverpool WMCA on Liverpool FC's development demonstrates an unconsidered connection, therefore, between the Merseyside club and that of the stridently Unionist Rangers. It has been argued by historians that the Glasgow club became a rallying point for men of Unionist sympathies because rivals Celtic had clearly come under the sway of directors who identified with the cause of Irish Home Rule.[30]

Clearly then there are similarities with the defining characteristics of the Glasgow "old Firm" experience and the relationship between the two Merseyside clubs at boardroom level from an ideological standpoint: with a number of Everton directors committed to Home Rule, and an even greater number of Liverpool FC men committed to Unionism. The simpatico of spirit between Liverpool FC and Glasgow Rangers FC in particular was personified in the form of the two men holding the reins of power at each club: Liverpool's John Houlding and Glasgow Rangers' longstanding chairman and majority shareholder, Sir John Ure Primrose. Both men were, in governance and financial terms, the central players in their respective clubs; each were fierce opponents of Irish Home Rule – Houlding through his connections with the Tory Party, Primrose through his position as a Liberal Unionist - and both were fiercely anti-socialist and anti-trade unionist. As we shall see in the following chapter, the two men also shared another thing in common: freemasonry.

Masonic Influence in the Boardroom of Liverpool FC

The act of becoming a freemason is quite common amongst middle class men, and especially those involved in business. Viewed now as a non-controversial and benign organisation focussed on charitable work, ostensibly freemasonry comes without the baggage of exclusion and discrimination. Freemasonry, however, started out as a vehicle for an elite stratum in British society and was viewed as separate, secretive and conspiratorial. By the late nineteenth and early twentieth centuries it had been transformed into a cross-class institution that encompassed not only the elite but also men from middle class trades and artisans, providing a crucial nexus for those holding the same socially conservative impulses. A common belief is that the masonic bond was also a means by which men of different social stripes who shared a commitment to Protestantism and a mutual mistrust and antagonism toward Catholics could come together. Further to this, it has been argued that freemasonry offered a means to exclude Catholics from positions of power and the betterment of their material conditions.

There was a historic antipathy between freemasonry and Catholicism which fuelled such discrimination. From the time of the Enlightenment the Catholic Church forbid Catholics from involvement in secret societies, viewing them as quasi-religious institutions and the type of organisations that held out the possibility of toppling the established ruling order in nations where Roman Catholicism was the officially recognised religion and where it held great social and political sway. In this reckoning the events of the French Revolution were to the fore and the part played in it by radical and revolutionary groups such as the sans-culottes and Jacobins.

For its part, freemasonry in Protestant nations viewed Catholicism with distrust and regarded with suspicion Roman Catholics for what they saw as their subservience to a foreign power – the Vatican. Freemasonry, in Britain, therefore, became identified as part of the Protestant Establishment: an institution that could be used to uphold Protestant values and maintain its dominance. In certain towns and cities of Britain marked by religious tensions, freemasonry is thought to have served as an institutional bulwark against Roman Catholics and a buttress of Protestant identity. This would certainly have been the case in places like Glasgow and Liverpool – cities with notorious levels of religious bigotry and fierce ethno-religious competition in the local job market.

Studies concerned with the sectarian divide of Glasgow football culture have long speculated about the significance of the role of freemasonry in the development of Glasgow Rangers Football Club. The aforementioned Sir John Ure Primrose established Masonic connections at Rangers in the late nineteenth century. Primrose was a prominent freemason: being elevated to the level of Grand Committee of the Grand Lodge of Scotland, the governing body of freemasonry north of the border, who initiated the formation of several lodges in Glasgow, including Plantation Lodge (581) and Pollock Lodge (722). It has been argued that freemasonry acted as a bonding agent at Rangers Football Club, ensuring loyalty to the club and the loyalty of the club to the Craft. In 1912 Primrose publicly pledged not only himself to the masonic cause but also the football club he controlled.[31] The known incompatibility of Catholicism with secret societies (and particularly freemasonry) meant that this declaration was interpreted as another means of excluding Roman Catholics from Rangers FC. This is a pertinent point to remember when considering the widespread influence of freemasonry at Liverpool FC.

Though the connection between Liverpool FC and Liverpool freemasonry was not as explicitly and publically stated as at Glasgow Rangers it nevertheless appears that men at the Merseyside club with boardroom ambitions would have found that it was important to be a freemason, or to become one in order to fulfil their ambition. At least this seems to have been the case in the period of the club's history dominated by its first chairman and majority share owner, John Houlding. Houlding had been a founding member of both Anfield Lodge (2213) and Sir Walter Raleigh Lodge (2837) he rose through the various levels of freemasonry from his first involvement with the craft in 1871, attaining the status of Provincial Grand Registrar and Provincial Grand Warden in West Lancashire by 1880. His masonic career reached its zenith in 1898 when becoming Grand Senior Deacon of England. Houlding was one of the few freemasons who attained the "33rd Degree" – the highest possible level any freemason can attain - an exclusive order within freemasonry restricted to seventy five members at any one point in time.[32] And from evidence uncovered it seems obvious that Houlding – seeking to populate the key positions of his new football club after experiencing open warfare with members of the committee in the old Everton club - turned not only toward his political allies but also his masonic brethren.

The influence of freemasons on all administrative posts at Liverpool FC was comprehensive. The positions of club president, chairman, directors, secretaries, managers and solicitors were all dominated by freemasons, and so too was the shareholder base of the club in its first decade and a half in existence. The very first annual general meeting in 1893 was overseen by a nine-man board comprising its president, John Houlding, chairman, Edwin Berry, treasurer, Richard H. Webster, secretary, William Barclay, and a directorate of John McKenna, John Asbury, John James Ramsey, William Houlding and John Dermot. Apart from the chairman's son, William Houlding, and Messrs. Barclay and Dermot, all the above named men were freemasons. So too were the club's solicitor Albert Edward Berry and auditors Simon Jude and Joseph West, men who would retain their positions and ties to the club until their deaths in the 1920s and 1930s. Of the forty-six original subscribers to the club in 1892 (a small figure only added to over the next decade by the careful selection of an extra handful of shareholders) twenty-one were freemasons.

This masonic grip upon the club hierarchy was consolidated as Liverpool reached the end of the Houlding era. In 1902 six of the eight directors were freemasons. John Houlding (now chairman), and directors John McKenna, John James Ramsey and John Asbury were joined on the board by fellow freemasons Edwin Berry, the former club treasurer, and Thomas Knowles, Houlding's son-in-law. By this point the club's first "imported" secretary-manager had been employed – Tom Watson, the successful ex-Sunderland manager, also a freemason. (See Appendix D for full details of masonic connections)

The club hierarchy at Liverpool and their small number of shareholders, then, were familiar to each other through a network of civic institutions: most prominently the Conservative Party and freemasonry. It appears that they preferred to keep the outside world at arm's length. And the club rules on taking up stock made this situation entirely possible. "New members shall be elected only at executive committee meetings and shall be duly proposed and seconded by two members of the executive", the club's Articles of Association determined.[33] The theory that the early Liverpool FC resembled something of a private gentleman's club rather than a sporting business gains traction when reading reports in the local sporting press from the period. 'The shareholders of Liverpool FC', stated the *Athletic News* in May 1899, 'are a few private gentlemen, who will meet when it pleases them, and let the public know just as much of their affairs as they may choose to communicate'. Later in that year the same journal (favourably comparing the Liverpool FC annual meeting with the traditionally more rambunctious Everton FC annual meetings) commented: 'When the harmony of the proceedings is compared with the wild behaviour at Everton's annual meeting, it is open to question whether, from some point of view, at any rate, a private football concern is not to be preferred to a public one. Liverpool FC are not likely to invite outside subscriptions just yet. The management is composed of a few wealthy gentlemen who prefer shouldering liabilities themselves to inviting the public to share them.'[34]

By adopting an invitation-only system of selection the number of shareholders at Liverpool FC remained extremely low. In the club's first seven years only eight new shareholders were added to the club. The total number of club members at the end of the nineteenth century stood at fifty-four. Of these, thirty-seven were either Conservative Party workers (just under half of the membership were involved in Conservative Party organizations of one description or another), freemasons or employed by the West Derby Union by John Houlding - the local poor law union he was the chief Guardian to. Under these conditions it can come as no surprise that freemasons would figure so prominently amongst the hierarchy of the club.

But the call for a greater number of subscriptions *did*

eventually come. The Houlding family in 1905, three years after the death of John Houlding, chose to end their association with the club, transferring to it their two-thirds majority stake in return for the club taking responsibility of a £5,000 overdraft taken out by the late chairman on behalf of Liverpool FC. This done, the sitting directors decided 'to place the Liverpool Football Club on a popular basis', as the club secretary described it in a match day programme. Share applications were sought and a public issue of the transferred Houlding shares plus two thousand newly created shares took place. Upon this act the number of shareholders rose from 64 in 1904 to 407 subscribers in 1905. Liverpool FC now had, like rivals Everton, a mass membership.

However, mass membership or not, there continued to be a dominance of positions of control at the club by men who were freemasons. In 1910, five years into the post-Houlding family era, the nine-man Liverpool FC board contained seven freemasons: erstwhile directors John McKenna, John James Ramsey and John Asbury were joined in the boardroom by new men who also involved in freemasonry: William Robert Williams, William Coward Briggs, Albert Worgan and Richard L Martindale. This numerical dominance lasted beyond the end of the First World War, as retiring freemason directors, or those dying while in office, were replaced in the period up until the early 1920s by other members of the Craft. Amongst these were James Herbert Troop, Thomas Bush and Fred Parry. And the death of secretary-manager Tom Watson in 1915 saw the hiring of yet another freemason, George Patterson, for that positon. It wasn't until the late 1920s and early 1930s that a marginalization of the masonic presence in the boardroom at Liverpool FC takes place.

It might have been expected with the departure from the scene of the all-powerful Houlding family – and more especially club founder, John Houlding with his prominent role in local, regional and national freemasonry circles – that the very high proportion of the club's hierarchy with Craft connections would have ebbed away rather than consolidate their presence in the Liverpool boardroom, as was the case. This counter intuitive development could perhaps partly be explained by assuming that existing directors had built up a considerable amount of status and social capital amongst the shareholders of the club which then transferred into the era of mass membership, allowing them to retain their seats in the boardroom. Some directors had been in their positions for a number of years, acquiring in the process a paternalistic aura that may have been translated into deference from a much larger body of shareholders when seeking re-election. This would account for the longevity of members of the board like John McKenna, John James Ramsey and John Asbury. However, it would not explain how many more new directors also from the masonic fraternity secured boardroom positions for the first time after 1905. A couple of other factors, therefore, may have to be taken into consideration in order to explain this continued dominant masonic presence.

One such factor relates to rule changes brought about relating to procedures for boardroom candidates. By special resolution at the June 1906 Extraordinary General Meeting a further article was added to the company's Articles of Association from 1892:

> No person, not being a retiring director, shall be eligible for the election to the office of director at any General Meeting unless he, or some other member proposing him, has, on or before the first day of May in the year in which such General Meeting is held, left at or sent to the registered office of the company a notice in writing duly signed, stating the full name and address of the candidate and either signifying his candidature for the office, or the intention of such member to propose him, in which latter case the name of the proposer and seconder shall be stated. [35]

It seems clear that the addition of these bureaucratic procedures were designed to both bring up to date for the era of mass membership earlier rules from the foundation of the club in 1892 concerning the powers of directors *and* to inhibit challenges to incumbent directors from the floor at club Annual General Meetings. Retiring incumbents of the post of club director (through procedure) could still automatically be part of the slate and seek re-election to the board. And an early and formalised declaration of a candidacy (involving nominee, nominator, and a seconder to this) benefits members seeking to gain entry to the board for the first time who have the guidance and support of "like-minded" sitting directors familiar with the bureaucratic procedures of club elections.

This brings forward another factor possibly at play: the influence of a small cluster of masonic lodges that tightly knitted together the large number of freemason directors at Liverpool FC already noted above. Three lodges in particular: Anfield Lodge (2213), Sincerity Lodge (292) and Everton Lodge (823) were the mother lodges of fifteen of the twenty-four freemasons to have served as directors and other members of the club hierarchy such as secretaries, treasurers etc, between 1892 and 1920. In many cases these men were masons in more than one of the three named lodges, displaying a great deal of overlap and integration with fellow directors outside of the football club. (See Appendix D). The concentration of so many club officials into this small number of lodges suggests that a well-worn path between them and the Liverpool boardroom had been established, and perhaps a co-ordinated strategy for selection was in place. It is instructive, therefore, that of the nine newly elected directors to the Liverpool

FC boardroom between 1905 and 1920 five of them were also freemasons at Anfield, Sincerity and Everton lodges. Even by 1920 five of the ten-man board were from these three lodges. If the extent of masonic involvement in the Liverpool FC hierarchy from its formation in 1892 is noteworthy, then the continued dominance of it by a small number of freemasons who were close associates within that fraternity is remarkable. This is more especially the case when considering that this dominance, as we have seen, stretches into an era at the club of mass shareholders, a flattening out of ownership and the greater scope for alternative slates of boardroom candidates to come forward for election.

§

The following section underlines the seniority of freemasons within Liverpool FC during the first three decades of its existence and their status within local, provincial and national freemasonry circles.

For all but eight years between 1892 and 1926 the chairmanship of Liverpool FC was held by freemasons John Houlding, Edwin Berry, John McKenna, John Asbury and Richard Lawson Martindale. Twenty of the thirty-six directors of the club who served on the board in the period 1892 to 1920 were freemasons. Freemasons exclusively carried out the administration of the legal and financial affairs of the club between 1892 and the early 1930s through solicitors Albert Edward Berry and Edwin Berry, and by auditors Simon Jude and Joseph West. In terms of on-field affairs the club's fortunes were also in the hands of freemasons. The aforementioned John McKenna was the club's first recognised secretary-manager (1894 to 1896). Succeeding McKenna (and at McKenna's insistence) was Tom Watson. Watson was in turn succeeded by George Patterson who took over the reins of team management until 1920, and again returning to that role from 1928 to 1936.

Being a freemason is not unusual to those involved football club administration, of course. Some of Britain's biggest clubs leave evidence of their connection to freemasonry. It has been mentioned already how Glasgow Rangers were closely associated with freemasonry by their most senior figure, Sir John Ure Primrose. And Manchester City's early pioneers have also been highlighted by historians as having particularly close links to the Craft. The Manchester club are said to have been founded by masons, transforming the club from St Marks FC to, eventually, Manchester City. Freemasons, in fact, had been at the helm of both the tributary clubs that eventually became Manchester City: St Marks FC and its successor, AFC Gorton.[36] One member of the Craft in particular, club secretary Joshua Parlby, has been credited with the rescue of Manchester City from financial ruin when the club were on the verge of bankruptcy in 1894. It is claimed the team colours of red and black were changed at this point to sky blue and white (colours synonymous with freemasonry) as an act of acknowledgement of his efforts.[37]

There is a claim too that Arsenal's freemason owner, Sir Henry Norris, marks that club out as an organization to be thought of as a club conspicuously associated with freemasonry. Norris, a Grand Deacon of the Grand Lodge of England, became a significant shareholder in Arsenal in 1910 and a domineering chairman of the club until his retirement in the early 1920s. Indeed, there are ties between the London club and Glasgow Rangers created under Norris' governance: shares in Arsenal were bought by Ranger's board of directors, led by Sir John Ure Primrose, *and* given to them by Henry Norris at a later point as a "thank you" to the Glasgow club for earlier financial assistance in straitened times at Arsenal.

However, despite these examples from other clubs, it is doubtful that such a comprehensive impact was made by freemasons in terms of ownership, control and influence at any major English or Scottish football club - and over such an extensive period - as that which occurred at Liverpool FC. It is a quite remarkable connection the club had with this institution. Even beyond the directors and various officers of the club, the small number of original subscribers also contained prominent freemasons. The most senior of these was Robert Wylie: a Grand

Deacon of England. So the Liverpool club could, through Robert Wylie's and John Houlding's place on the Council of the Grand Lodge of England, boast a very significant connection to the national ruling body of the Craft.

Further to this, it should be mentioned that the Liverpool FC masonic fellowship were also noteworthy in terms of the high-honours they gained in Provincial freemasonry. The credentials of the club's founder, John Houlding, with regard to his status within freemasonry tends to overshadow the achievements of all other freemasons at the club. However, other men within the Liverpool hierarchy were prominent within the local and regional Craft fraternity. It is routine to read in the biographical accounts and obituaries of these men the term "prominent freemason". Many were masons at more than one lodge and most had become Worshipful Masters of at least one lodge – the highest ranking position within it. Some were responsible for creating new lodges, as did Edwin Berry and Thomas Bush.

However, the involvement of club officials in freemasonry went beyond the local lodge. Besides John Houlding, eight other directors of the club were promoted to Provincial Rank. Provincial Grand Lodges consisted of a group of between thirty to forty masons chosen to oversee masonic affairs at a, roughly, county-wide level. Those elevated to Provincial rank were required to have been 'through the chair' – that is, been made Worshipful Master of their Mother lodge. In short, those chosen to step up to county-wide organisational level were considered 'high fliers' at a local level. All of the eight Liverpool FC directors reaching Provincial Grand Lodge were promoted to the rank of Provincial Grand Senior Deacon. Richard Lawson Martindale, John James Ramsey, John McKenna, William C. Briggs, Simon Jude, Robert Henry Webster were Provincial Grand Deacons at West Lancashire Grand Lodge, and Albert E. Berry and his brother Edwin Berry at Cheshire Grand Lodge.

The principal duties of the Senior Deacon are to conduct newly promoted freemasons around the Provincial Lodge, to speak up for them during ceremonies, and also to attend the Grand Master when required and to carry out his orders. They are, in essence, the messengers of the Grand Master. And we can perhaps gain an understanding about the character of the men of the Liverpool FC boardroom from this information. On the one hand, they exhibit the ambition to make the leap from local to provincial status – no doubt under the guidance of one of the most senior freemasons in the country who happened to sit side by side with them in the club boardroom. On the other hand, there came - through their masonic duties - a mindfulness of one's responsibility to those in an organisation both above and below in rank. Ambitions are tempered by group loyalty and by deference. These attributes could be usefully replicated in a football club setting: creating a sense of duty to the organisation as a whole, a sense of camaraderie between board members, and due deference to senior members of that board. It might also be said that the process of moving through the ranks prepared fellow freemasons in the Liverpool membership for a transition to the boardroom.

§

When considered alongside the Unionist and Orange politics of many senior members of the club, it is reasonable to suggest that the extensive connections at Liverpool FC to freemasonry (a quasi-religious institution completely at odds with the Roman Catholic church - hostile toward it and those devoted to it) are a pointer to core values which would likely have prevailed. They would have helped create a common ethos at the helm of that organization in its crucial formative period *and* contributed toward a sectarian identity being established in the Liverpool boardroom. [38]

Identification with Different Ethnic and Religious Groups at Everton and Liverpool Football Clubs?

If in an earlier period of their development there was a clear and demonstrable difference in attitude toward religious and political affairs between the Merseyside clubs at boardroom level, did this lay the basis for them to appeal to distinct ethno-religious audiences or to *operate* along sectarian lines? I think, overall, the answer to this question is that they did not, although the matter is a complex one which I shall return to later below. Certainly, the scope was there for the two clubs to capitalise and prosper on a sectarian business model. In a number of Scottish and Northern Irish towns religious and political leaders took the crucial lead in the development of professional football organisations. They viewed football clubs as a form of cultural capital able to consolidate religious and ethnic identity. This was especially the case in relation to the efforts of the Irish Catholic hierarchy in those locations. In Liverpool, however, a city also riven with sectarian tensions, such a sporting lead was not forthcoming. The establishment of separate football organization was not a priority. Rather, a "denationalisation" process was encouraged by the Liverpool Catholic Church who were anxious to blur Irish-British identities in accordance with its main aim of the integration of their congregation into this most hostile of cities.[39]

Despite this, some in the Liverpool Irish community *did* attempt to form their own football organisations; Liverpool 5th Irish football club is probably the most high profile example of these efforts. The team's origins lay in the 5th Irish Volunteer Rifle Brigade, a body of men recruited exclusively from the Liverpool Irish Catholic community. "The Irishmen" as they became known were formed in 1888 in the Everton district and played their football competitively in the Liverpool and District Amateur League and West Lancashire and District League. The club, however, failed to connect with the local Irish community and were disbanded in 1894 without ever commanding a large following. A host of other clubs designated "Hibernian" and "Celtic" were formed and stepped forward into the field of play, along with parish teams such as the Old Xaverians (an outgrowth of St Francis Xavier college in Everton). But most of these clubs were relatively short lived and had an inauspicious playing record. So fleeting was their existence that little record is left of them, save for a few score lines of their games which survive in snippets in the local press. None could claim to have been embraced by the local Irish community in the manner that some Irish clubs in Scotland and Northern Ireland had been during this same period. Efforts at setting up specifically ethno-religious football clubs in Liverpool were not pursued with much vigour.[40]

Under these circumstances the established professional football clubs of Liverpool stood to profit by judicious appeals to different religious communities by indulging in the type of carve up of the local football market associated with the Old Firm clubs of Glasgow. If this were to have been a model the Merseyside clubs wanted to adopt, one of the levers they might have pulled would have been to follow a recruitment policy that encouraged the signing of players from a particular background (or, putting it another way, a policy of excluding players from a particular background) as was the case with Glasgow Rangers or the Belfast club, Linfield. An "unwritten policy" of not signing Roman Catholic players was in place at those clubs until well into the latter decades of the twentieth century, and this became a crucial strategy in securing a sectarian duopoly that could command supporter loyalty – assembling before supporters playing staff they could identify with. In the case of Glasgow Rangers this went as far as the marginalisation of players within the club who had married Roman Catholics.

Ironically, an argument often used by those defending the Merseyside clubs from the charge of sectarianism has been to highlight Everton's signing of Irish-born players as an explanation for the "confusion" over religious links attributed to the two Liverpool teams – as if this flow of talent could not be used as evidence to the contrary. In the mid-twentieth century Everton forged connections with clubs in Ireland, such as Dundalk and with Dublin teams Shamrock Rovers and Shelbourne. These links reaped a harvest of players, such as Tommy Clinton, Peter Corr, Tommy Eglington, Peter Farrell, Jimmy O'Neill, George Cummins, Dan Donovan, Mick Meagan and Jimmy Sutherland. The employment of former Manchester United captain and Irish international John Carey as manager in 1958 gave the team a distinctive "Hibernian" flavour - a point made by former Everton player Brian Harris in his biography, and in a not entirely complimentary fashion.[41] However, well before that era Everton had established a frequent supply line in Irish talent: a connection so rich as to be described as an 'Eireann tradition'.[42] The first signing from Ireland was Jack Kirwan, a player plucked from Gaelic Football outfit St James Gaels in 1898. Kirwan's move to Goodison was followed by Shelbourne team mates Valentine Harris (another convert from Gaelic Football) and Billy Lacey – men who went on to manage the Irish Free State national team in the 1930s. Other notable Irish internationals that went on to play for Everton were Billy Scott, Belfast Celtic's Jackie Coulter and Alex Stevenson. Probably for this reason Everton were the first English club to have a supporters' association set up in Ireland, becoming the first example of a club with a large "overseas" support, as hundreds of Irishmen travelled to Liverpool for Everton games. Symbolically, the connection between Everton and Ireland was cemented with the move of Everton's greatest ever player and iconic figure, William Ralph (*Dixie*) Dean, to Sligo Rovers in 1939; Dean going on to win the Irish Cup with Rovers in the 1939/40 season.

By contrast, Ireland was a virtually untapped market for Liverpool FC until the end of the twentieth century. During the 1980s Liverpool signed a host of Irish international stars including Ronnie Whelan, Steve Staunton, Jim Beglin and Michael Robinson. This conspicuously late influx of Irishmen into the club has led some to talk of a less welcoming attitude toward Irish-born players at Liverpool FC than traditionally was extended to them by their near-neighbours. Given the clearly hostile attitude toward Irish Catholics from men in control of Liverpool FC in its foundational period it would be difficult to deny that the possibility existed at the club of a policy of non-employment of men from Catholic Ireland. However, a more benign explanation for this disparity might be found in the initial scouting networks set up by Liverpool FC. Through the club's first secretary-manager, John McKenna, Liverpool from their inception targeted proven players of quality out of necessity as a newly formed club needing to hit the ground running. This meant, essentially, a turn toward players from Scotland - a traditional route followed by ambitious English clubs seeking professional players during this period. McKenna immediately signed thirteen Scots professionals from which were constructed the celebrated "team of macs" of the early 1890s. Scotland had a deep well of talent that McKenna returned to in his years as club secretary-manager, and it became a scouting pattern which his successors kept faith with over the years. Thus, a tradition was set in place. In the words of one Liverpool fan:

> Liverpool FC has been blessed with the impressive contributions of many nationalities down the years, but the impact of Scottish players and managerial staff is arguably unequalled at Anfield...Liverpool's history is built on the shoulders of Scottish players and their grit, skill, determination and excellent leadership and motivational ability.[43]

Some of the most celebrated players in the club's history have made the journey from Scotland to Anfield including Alex Raisbeck, Ted Doig, Billy Liddell, Ian St.John, Ron Yeats, Kenny Dalglish and Graeme Souness. It has been argued that this heavy bias toward recruitment north of the border inculcated the club with 'a robust Scottish Protestant ethic'.[44] The fact that this Scottish recruitment included players from both sides of the religious divide, though, - Catholic *and* Protestant - casts doubt on the validity of stressing the sectarian importance of the sourcing of players from "Presbyterian Scotland" rather than "Catholic Ireland". The earliest Liverpool teams also included many players transferred from Scots-Irish clubs who were of Irish Catholic descent, such as Andy McGuigan from Hibernian and James McBride and Joseph McQue from Glasgow Celtic. And the celebrated Manchester United manager, Matt

Busby, signed by Liverpool in 1935 and made club captain soon after, was a devout Roman Catholic from an Irish-Scots background.

There have also been claims suggesting that, over time, the Merseyside clubs operated an informal city-based scouting arrangement along religious lines. Specifically, this was said to have worked on the basis of Everton and Liverpool casting their net over promising young players within the city's schoolboy representative teams. The theory goes that Everton were given the opportunity of choosing the cream of local Catholic talent; Liverpool were allowed free rein to do the same with state schooled or Protestant schooled boys.[45] It was noted earlier in this volume that Catholic clerics especially were set in their judgement over the matter of "proper" choices of football clubs for boys with promise. And there is anecdotal evidence suggesting a firm belief amongst Liverpool youngsters interested in football that Everton and Liverpool were hospitable or unhospitable destinations for them, depending on their religious background – a perception fueled in some cases by school teachers.[46] This theory regarding local scouting networks, however informally operated, remains a matter of speculation. What we can say with confidence, though, and certainly in the post-Second World war period, is that, contrary to the proposed model, many players brought up in the Liverpool-Irish community had little problem in becoming Liverpool players. In the 1950s and 1960s boys from Catholic backgrounds such as Bobby Campbell, Jimmy Melia, Chris Lawler, Tommy Smith and Gerry Byrne were signed by Liverpool FC and went on to be highly successful professional players. In fact, Byrne was signed up for Liverpool whilst playing for the Liverpool Catholic Schoolboys team, which suggests that – at least by this point – any apparent "carving up" of local emerging talent along sectarian lines had been dismissed as a functioning model.

§

Beyond player recruitment policy, another way that the Merseyside clubs could have profited from stressing differing identities and traditions would have been by forging exclusive associations with particular religious or ethnic organisations. Did differences here provide substance for the claimed Catholic-Protestant religious labels attached to each of the Merseyside clubs? Again, we can go back to the example of Scottish football where such tactics were employed to secure and reinforce support from separate ethno-religious communities. Glasgow Rangers' association with the Orange Order, for instance, underlined their Protestant and Unionist credentials. On occasion, the Glasgow club offered its Ibrox Stadium as a venue for the annual religious service held by the Glasgow Province's Orange Lodges and allowed its team to play benefit matches in Northern Ireland for a variety of Orange Order charities. For their part Rangers' rivals Celtic emphasised their role as a totem of Irish Catholic cultural identity in the city by, for example, making its founding principle the provision of charity for the Catholic poor and by allowing their ground, Celtic Park, to be used for the holding of Roman Catholic mass on important feast days in the religious calendar and opening up use of the stadium for musical occasions that were clearly culturally Irish.[47]

This state of affairs does not seem to have been repeated on Merseyside. All available evidence points toward a non-partisan approach to community relations by the clubs, with neither Everton or Liverpool predominantly favouring one particular religious or ethnic denomination over another. For example, the Liverpool Catholic schools' annual sports days were hosted alternately at Goodison Park and Anfield in the Inter War period. And another institution enjoying the patronage of both clubs was The League of Welldoers: a charity set up in the Victorian period at Limekiln Lane, off Scotland Road in the heart of "Irish Liverpool". Also known as 'Lee Jones" after its philanthropist founder, the charity provided a crucial intervention in the pre-welfare state era amongst the poor and destitute. Everton FC regularly hosted food parties and organized games for children sent by the charity, whilst Liverpool director Richard L. Martindale was one of the League's governors.

Both Everton and Liverpool football clubs also appear to have been on friendly terms with the premier Catholic college in Liverpool: St Francis Xavier. Both clubs gave assistance to St Francis Xavier's by providing coaches to help train their various sporting teams. Everton player and future club director, Daniel Kirkwood, and Liverpool player, Alex McCowie, were seconded to Saint Francis Xavier as football coaches.[48]

Such outreach efforts were not restricted to the Catholic community. In the pre Second World War period the players and management of Everton and Liverpool took part jointly in services held by Nonconformist congregations. These so-called 'Football Sundays' were formal affairs, often with a civic dignitary in attendance and directors and players from each club called upon to speak. More typical of Everton and Liverpool's community support, however, was their aiding of secular causes, such as alms giving to local hospitals. Stanley Hospital in the Kirkdale district of Liverpool in particular was the frequent recipient of financial donations from both clubs. They also appear to have taken an interest in alleviating the hardship of the local labour force in periods of economic downturn. In 1895, at the height of a bleak winter of trade inactivity in the port, Everton donated £1000 to relief agencies and set up a soup kitchen to provide for 12,000 people. And in 1905 both clubs agreed to donate a third of the gate receipts from the Liverpool

Senior Cup final to the city's Unemployed Fund (although the extent of the Liverpool board's good will in this respect is questioned by their later refusal to allow matchday collections for striking Liverpool dockworkers).[49]

Conclusion

Is there any substance, then, to the assertion that religious differences have played a significant part in the history of the Merseyside clubs? That was the question posed at the beginning of this volume. Perhaps a judicious conclusion to make would be that, though there is no compelling argument to make the case that football on Merseyside *exactly* followed the path taken in Glasgow, Edinburgh or Belfast, there *was* in some very interesting and important respects a distinct identity cleavage between the two Liverpool clubs that mirrors football's development in those places and most definitely *does* warrant acknowledgement.

It has been shown that the patterns of control at each club in the late Victorian and Edwardian period were startling in their difference. In particular, the social and political contrast between the men populating the boardrooms at each club would not look out of place when comparing the hierarchy of Glasgow's Old Firm or that of, say, Belfast Celtic with Linfield FC. This identity cleavage could have been of enormous importance for the development of football in the city. Historians chronicling the development of football clubs associated with religious sectarianism in Scotland and Northern Ireland, for example, are firm in their opinion that the identities of these clubs are less a result of their being initially founded as sporting outgrowths of a particular church or chapel denomination than they are the product of long established boardroom hierarchies who stamp them in their own image. Clubs like Glasgow Celtic, Hibernian and Belfast Celtic, founded initially to provide charity to the Catholic poor and as an outreach to young Catholic men, soon found their direction dictated by a local business elite, many of whom were involved in Irish Nationalist politics. Similarly, the identity of Glasgow Rangers and Linfield – clubs which, if not being founded by Presbyterian chapels, had their roots within that religious tradition – were molded most tellingly of all by the Unionist politics of men who dominated their boardrooms.[50]

For this reason alone, the claims of a religious schism in Merseyside football cannot simply be dismissed as the product of some supporters looking for convenient binary opposites, as it all too often has been in official club accounts and by commentators. Historian Raymond Boyle, for example, has argued that 'the origins of the two biggest clubs in Liverpool are important in understanding how neither club became closely associated with a specific community in the city'. Quite obviously, and as we have seen, this is a complete misreading of the situation based, I would suggest, on a lack of archival research on the men in control of the two football clubs and a lack of contextual analysis of the Merseyside social and political landscape of the period that they operated in. A similar misunderstanding of the founding fathers of Merseyside professional football and an under-appreciation of the connective tissue of this sectarian city's body politic is on display when sports historian Tony Mason states that 'there was nothing in the differences which produced Liverpool out of Everton which could remotely be classed religious'. Matters of religion and ethnicity were, in fact, to the fore in the splitting of the original Everton club *and* in the relations of those men who went on to control the two new club companies for years after that tumultuous event of 1892. This is because religion was tightly bound up with their political differences - differences so fierce that they could no longer be contained in the one sporting body.[51]

Context is all important here. Against the backdrop of the agitation for Irish Home Rule, the identity of the quite clearly Protestant-Unionist pioneering generation of men at Liverpool FC was based on an aggressive antagonism toward Irish self-determination and Roman Catholicism. This hostile attitude, as we have seen, was articulated on occasion by major figures in the Liverpool FC boardroom. By contrast, the avowedly pro-Home Rule sympathies of an influential core of Everton directors involved in Liberal politics (and men who moved in Irish Nationalist circles within the city), placed them fundamentally at odds with their counterparts on the Liverpool FC board and locates their identity outside of a British Imperialist framework (unquestionably concerning Ireland's future within that framework).

It might be expected then that such obvious political differences in leadership would impact on the running of the clubs in the same fashion that the football clubs of Glasgow or Belfast were so influenced. In terms of player acquisition there *were* interesting differences in the targeting and recruitment of players. Everton's forging of strong links with Ireland could be argued to be a follow on from its early boardroom profile. And any such "policy" might explain the sizeable anecdotal evidence professing Everton to be a team supported by Liverpool Catholics: the theory being that the large amount of Irish players the club attracted to it helped ignite a certain degree of "ethnic pride" in Everton amongst the city's Irish-born or those of Irish descent. One writer with knowledge of both the early Glasgow and Merseyside professional football scenes believed this to have been the case. 'Everton Football Club, like Celtic Football Club', wrote Celtic historian, James Handley, 'owed its success to immigrant support, the Irish in Liverpool rallying wholeheartedly round it'.[52] If so, this could also have been a shrewd early move on the part of Everton's directors to corner the as-yet-to-be exploited spectator market of less skilled elements of Liverpool's working class, which overwhelmingly the Liverpool Irish would have fallen into at this time.

However, despite there being a marked difference between Everton and Liverpool in the volume of players selected from Ireland (and, conversely, from "Presbyterian Scotland"), evidence suggests that, overall, there appears to have been no attempt by the clubs to operate discriminatory policies on the grounds of religious sectarianism when employing playing staff. We saw how the earliest Liverpool teams included many players from Catholic backgrounds – local and imported players. Neither does there appear to have been any policy to build up support amongst one section of the population to the exclusion of support from another section. It is concluded, broadly, that a non-partisan approach toward community relations were fostered by both clubs. There was no obvious effort made to secure a support base by repeating the type of divisive practices via "community outreach programmes" based on ethno-religious lines found in certain other football cultures elsewhere in similarly sectarian-torn parts of Britain - nor, indeed, to mirror the divisions found in the City of Liverpool on every level at this point in time: from schooling to housing; from welfare provision to workplace recruitment. This latter point may have prompted the Liverpool Lord Mayor's observation in 1933 that the two clubs had done more 'to cement good fellowship...than anything said or done in the last 25 years' - a period blighted by sectarian unrest in the city.[53]

On balance, it can be said that the conditions *did* exist to divide up football support in Liverpool along ethno-religious lines in the late nineteenth century and early twentieth century, should there have been an attempt to do so. The failure or refusal of the leadership of Irish Liverpool to support or sponsor a challenger organization to the major professional clubs in the city did not completely shut down the possibility of football in Liverpool taking this decidedly sectarian turn. It seems evident that under these circumstances Everton FC became a surrogate club for Irish Catholics seeking to identify with, and give their support to, a professional football club - even though that club's early complex history as one created by the host community and governed for the most part by members of that host community ensured that Everton would never easily be identified as a club with a *distinct* Irish Catholic identity.

On the other side of the divide, John Houlding was deeply suspicious of "radicalism", Liberalism and Roman Catholicism, and the men he as majority shareholder and chairman of Liverpool FC chose to surround himself with bears testimony to his determination to repel their advance within his orbit of influence. Even without the counter-weight of an *explicitly* "Catholic" civic football rival, it is entirely possible that Houlding's passing at the beginning of the twentieth century saved the Liverpool football scene from taking a decidedly Glaswegian turn, as the levels of sectarian violence were ramped up to dangerous levels in the city and groups of young men, as in other towns and cities blighted by religious discrimination, cast about for symbols to bolster their ethno-religious allegiances.

When the Houlding era ended at Liverpool FC there was the scope for the complete domination of a sectarian identity in the boardroom to come to an end. After his death in 1902 and the selling up of the Houlding family shares three years later, Liverpool FCs hierarchy saw a gradual dilution of their earlier Protestant-Unionist identity and a more balanced social profile to the club took shape. The election and appointment of men to positions of power at Liverpool FC that would never have been countenanced at an earlier point. Men like Roman Catholics Thomas Crompton and Joseph John Hill, for example, who were elected to the Liverpool board just prior to the First World War, confirms this reconfiguration. Although the Reds of Liverpool retained their True Blue hierarchy for years to come,[54] the more aggressive Orange political hue of the leadership of its formative period was tempered sufficiently to see off the danger of the club becoming for decades longer the redoubt of men implacable in their support for

Protestant Unionism and exclusive of anyone not firm in their belief of that cause.

§

In a city that devours all aspects of their football clubs' past exploits and chronicles their heroes lives with meticulous attention to detail, there has been an incredible void regarding the impact John Houlding had on football's foundation in Liverpool – and on Liverpool FCs history in particular. Such was the controversially exclusive nature of his reign that the present day Liverpool FC barely acknowledge Houlding's crucial role in the history of their club, much less celebrate it. There are no statues or dedicated books for a man who bestrode the professional game in Liverpool in its earliest decades, such is his toxicity for modern football clubs who thrive only as a result of their inclusivity and their ability to appeal across all social groups. Any mention of his name, or that of his chosen coterie of directors and club officers and their role in the club's foundation, are brief and shorn of context. There appears to be a willful ignorance of the milieu that Houlding and his club allies operated in and the impact that would likely have had on Liverpool FCs early identity. Houlding was known during his adult life by the soubriquet "King John". He is, though, the largely forgotten monarch – and perhaps for some, a best forgotten one.

Appendices

<u>Appendix A: Anecdotal Evidence Regarding Merseyside Football Ethno-Religious Schism</u>

Over the years there has been a substantial amount of anecdotes regarding what is seen to be a sectarian divide between Everton and Liverpool football clubs. Below are a selection of comments and observations from a variety of people – artists, clerics, journalists, as well as every day Liverpudlians - that articulate this view.

§

'The original club schism was said to have been about the rent. But, more likely, it had undertones of a religious war, such as there exists between Celtic and Rangers. To some extent, the divisions are still there – Everton, the Catholics, Liverpool, the Protestants. Staff and players were at one-time subject to sectarian vetting, but all that has long since been forgotten in Liverpool' - Composer, Fritz Speigl. *The Listener*, June 2nd 1977.

'The Catholic symbolism of clubs such as Everton, Manchester United and Celtic is still strong' – Steven Redhead, *Football with Attitude*. p.20 (1991)

'People 'dressed' their houses to advertise Cup Final footballing allegiances, though my Mum would never allow my brother's Evertonian blue to go up in case neighbours or passers-by mistakenly took us for Catholics' – John Williams (football sociologist) *Into the Red: Liverpool FC and the Changing Face of English Football* (2002) p.10

'It was strange in the 1930s for a Catholic to support Liverpool' – John Woods (Liverpool author) *Growin' Up: One Scouser's Social History of Liverpool* (2007) p.43

'In Liverpool, even in the two-ups and two-downs, most Protestants were Conservative and most Catholics were Labour, just as Everton was the Catholic team and Liverpool the Proddy-Dog one' – Cilla Black (singer). *Liverpool Echo* December 17th 2002

'Being a Roman Catholic school, religion played a large part in our school life. Pop Moran even tried to turn me off football at Anfield – Catholics were traditionally Everton supporters and players, Liverpool were the Protestant team. Pop honestly thought that being a Catholic I wouldn't be happy at Anfield' – Tommy Smith (ex Liverpool FC player and captain) *I Did It the Hard Way* (1980) p.14

'Everton Football Club, like Celtic Football Club', wrote Celtic historian, James Handley, 'owed its success to immigrant support, the Irish in Liverpool rallying wholeheartedly round it' – James E Handley (Roman Catholic priest). *The Celtic Story: A History of the Celtic Football Club* (1960)

'The Blood of the Martyrs Catholic Church – named according to the local priest, Father Inch, because Catholicism in this part of England was maintained by the blood of the martyrs – is where Wayne Rooney was baptised and confirmed a Catholic – an Irish Catholic. Father Inch is a Toffee true and true. Everton Football Club is the Irish team in Liverpool and it's no surprise therefore, that Rooney is a Blue' - David McWilliams (journalist) 'HiBrits: Ireland's Loss, England's Gain' (July 9th 2007)
http://www.davidmcwilliams.ie/2007/07/09/hibrits-irelands-loss-englands-gain

'Mary's family were Catholics so they automatically supported Everton. But anybody who wanted to be associated with success and elegant football would have backed Everton anyway because they were much the better team, lording it over the top of the division, their ground Goodison Park rising high above Stanley Park' - Alexei Sayle (comedian). Extract from his novel *Barcelona Plates* (2000) p.203

'It was an odd building, originally used for balls and dances with a severe neoclassical exterior and no windows giving it the appearance of a large mausoleum, decorated inside with Irish Republican and Everton FC memorabilia' – comedian Alexei Sayle writing about the Liverpool Irish Centre in his biography *Thatcher Stole my Shoes* (2016) p.136

'"If You're Feeling Tired and Lonesome" is another traditional song. As Liverpool had the tradition of being the Protestant club years ago a lot of their tunes are linked to marching songs, the type you'd hear on July 12th':

If you're tired and you're weary,
And your heart skips a beat,
You'll get your fucking head kicked in,
If you walk down Heyworth Street,
If you come to The Albert,
You'll hear our famous noise,
Get out you Everton bastards,
We're the Billy Shankly Boys

We're the boys from The Kop,
We're loyal and we're true,
And when we play the Everton,
We're ready for a do,
With a cry of "no surrender",
You'll hear our famous noise,
Get out you Everton bastards,
We're the Billy Shankly Boys

Peter Hooton (singer, The Farm) 'Peter Hooton's Kop Top 20' (2007) http://lfcimages.com/news/latest-news/peter-hooton-s-kop-top-20 lyrics from Liverpool FC Songs, *Anfield Online* https://www.anfield-online.co.uk/features/lfcsongs.htm

'Until Mr Bugler, casually and effortlessly, dropped it into one of his enticing monologues about the Blues, none of us had ever heard of any connection between Everton and the Roman Catholic Church nor Liverpool and the Protestant Church...nonchalantly he had supported his statement with the observation that all three parish priests were keen Evertonians, as was Archbishop Heenan. He had even hinted at a link between Everton and Pope Pious...We asked questions when we got home. The answers confirmed what Mr Bugler had seemingly innocuously told us. Everton were indeed regarded as a Catholic club and Liverpool a Protestant one' – Alan Edge (Liverpool author) speaking of his Liverpool childhood from the early 1950s in *Faith of our Fathers* (1997) pp.97-98

'Liverpool the Protestant team, beat Everton the Catholic team by 6-1 and Pat says to Mick "Aye, there'll be some sad hearts in the Vatican tonight"' - Arthur Askey (Liverpool Comedian) *Before Your Very Eyes* (1975) pp.34-35

'In the June of 1960 John [Moores] became chairman of Everton. Surprise has been expressed over the years that he should have chosen what some regard as a Catholic team in preference to the Protestant team, Liverpool, in which he also had shares' – Barbara Clegg, author of Sir John Moores' biography *The Man Who Made Littlewoods* (1993), p.183. Moores was a man who served on the City Council as a staunch Conservative for many years.

'Ethnic identity is real. One of the most intractable ethnic feuds in modern British community life, that of Catholics versus Protestants, still plays out in football rivalry, a kind of tribal warfare. Witness the football clubs Everton and Liverpool, Catholic and Protestant rivals in Liverpool...not to forget Celtic and Rangers in Glasgow' - *Catholic Herald*, November 24th 2006

'While waiting to go into the Kop for the European Cup semi-final against Zurich on 20th April 1977 I had just started going to Anfield after coming down from Scotland, where I supported Celtic. There were two middle-aged men behind me, and one of them got a Rangers scarf out of his pocket and put it on. The other one said, "you're as safe as houses in there with that on". It hit me then: "Is Liverpool a Rangers supporters' club?"' – Liverpool fan, Billy Wilson quoted in Steven F Kelly, *The Kop: End of an Era* (1993) p.53

'One Liverpool fan...born and raised a Catholic, attributes his deviation from the rule to a rebellious father whose twelve older siblings had all followed the blue party line. Many fans of both teams are aware of this unwritten tradition, whether they conform to it or not. Even as recently as November 1988, a piece of graffiti scrawled above a turnstile at the Anfield Road end read: "No Fenian Twats". A city's bigotry does not die overnight' - Dave Hill, biographer of John Barnes *Out of His Skin: The John Barnes Story*, (1989). pp.68-69

Appendix B: Glossary of Terms and Organisations

Organisations

Gladstonian Liberal Party – an informal name given to the bulk of the Liberal Party who remained loyal to their leader, William Ewart Gladstone, in the wake of his adoption of the Irish Home Rule – an event which saw a split and the creation of the Liberal Unionists, who opposed Home Rule.

Grand Lodge of England - the highest masonic authority in English freemasonry

Irish Nationalist League – a political organization formed in Liverpool in the 1870s to further the interests of Irish Catholics in municipal affairs

Laymen's League – a Protestant pressure group that promoted policy based on theology. Responsible in the nineteenth century for promoting so called Church Discipline Bills to be read in parliament

League of Welldoers – a charitable organization carrying out relief effort in the heart of "Irish Liverpool"

Liverpool Conservative and Unionist Party – the full name of the British Conservative Party

Liverpool Parliamentary Debating Society – a political debating society created in Liverpool in the nineteenth century designed to "shadow" the major political parties and discuss the major issues of the day

National Protestant Union – an Evangelical Anglican body committed to helping political candidates at elections who upheld the principles of the Protestant Reformation

Orange Order – a largely working class Protestant religious organization committed to the union of Britain and Ireland

Provincial Grand Lodge – the highest masonic authority in a British geographical region (usually county-wide)

West Derby Union – a poor law union in Liverpool (the biggest in England at the time period under discussion in this volume) responsible for administering alms, medical provision and shelter to the poorest and most destitute in society

Working Men's Conservative Association – a cross-class, quasi-religious political organization set up by the Liverpool Conservative Party to advance their appeal to the city's Protestant working class

Terms

Denationalisation – in respect to this volume, the denial of the study or celebration of their Irish ancestry for the Liverpool Irish community, particularly by the Liverpool Catholic Archdiocese

Disloyalists – a pejorative term used by Conservative Unionists to denounce the Home Rule supporting Gladstonian wing of the Liberal Party

Freemasonry (The Craft) – a quasi-religious fraternity. To its adherents an institution which offers mutual assistance and brotherly love; to its detractors a secretive and conspiratorial society

Irish Home Rule – a nineteenth and early twentieth century political policy designed to peacefully agitate via parliament for Irish independence and which united British Liberals with Irish nationalists

Irish Liverpool – those people either born in Ireland or are/were the descendants of immigrant Irish who settled in Liverpool, particularly the dockside communities of Scotland Road and Vauxhall

Irish Nationalism – an ideology committed to the establishment of Irish independence from Britain

Old Firm – a term used in relation to the mutually strengthening rivalry of Glasgow Celtic and Glasgow Rangers

Radicals – a term usually used by Conservatives as a pejorative for any social or political force outside of the Conservative Party perceived to hold view threatening to the status quo

Ritualism – usually used as a pejorative by militant Protestants who oppose what they see as the dilution of Protestantism by the reintroduction into Anglican church services of the trappings of Roman Catholic worship

Popery – a pejorative term for Roman Catholics used by politically motivated Protestant groups

Sectarian – in the context of this volume discrimination between the Liverpool Irish Catholic and Protestant communities

The split of 1892 – the division of the Everton football club that had existed as a members club between 1879 and 1892

Ulster Unionists – a political movement encompassing people on either side of the Irish Sea who defend the rights of the people of the north of Ireland to maintain their political link to Britain

33rd Degree – an exclusive order within freemasonry that only a handful of masons ever achieve in their careers

Appendix C: Politically Active Directors who were Protagonists in the early Development of Everton and Liverpool Football Clubs

Everton FC:

William Robert Clayton. Chairman of Formby Liberal Association.

Dr James Clement Baxter. Surgeon and Liberal city councilor for Liverpool's St. Anne's ward.

Alfred Gates. Alderman, Sandhills ward. Leader of the Liberal Party in Liverpool City Council.

George Mahon, Everton's first chairman, was a committee member of Walton Liberal Association.

Arthur Riley Wade. Member of Liverpool Exchange Liberal Association.

Dr William Whitford. Chairman of Everton and Kirkdale Liberal Association.

Liverpool FC:

Benjamin E. Bailey. Chairman of West Derby Conservative Association. Secretary of Liverpool Workingmen's Conservative Association. Mayor of Bootle.

Albert Edward Berry. Chairman Liverpool Conservative Club. Solicitor Liverpool Workingmen's Conservative Association.

Edwin Berry. Conservative Councillor, Breckfield ward. Solicitor Liverpool Workingmen's Conservative Association.

John Houlding. Conservative Alderman, Everton and Kirkdale ward. Liverpool Workingmen's Conservative Association executive committee.

William Houlding. Conservative Councillor, Anfield ward.

Simon Jude. Conservative Alderman, Netherfield ward. Liverpool Workingmen's
Conservative Association executive committee.

James McCracken. Deputy Grand Master Liverpool Loyal Orange Institution.

John McKenna. Liverpool Constitutional Association.

Ephraim Walker. Conservative Alderman, St Domingo ward. Liverpool Workingmen's Conservative Association executive committee.

Richard H Webster. Liverpool Workingmen's Conservative Association. St Domingo ward branch committee member.

James A. Willox. Conservative MP Everton. President of the National Protestant Association.

Appendix D: Liverpool FC's Freemason Hierarchy, 1892-1920
(source Grand Lodge of England Country Returns – and, where mentioned, local press reports)

Acronym key:

LC - *Liverpool Courier*
LDP - *Liverpool Daily Post*
LM - Liverpool Mercury
GLCR - *Grand Lodge Country Returns*

John Asbury – Marlborough Lodge (1620) LDP Jan 22nd 1914

Albert Edward Berry - Everton Lodge (823), Wallasey Lodge (3036) LDP Feb 27th 1931

Edwin Berry – Sefton Lodge (680), Wilbraham Lodge (1713) LDP Nov 23rd 1925

William Coward Briggs - Everton Lodge (823), Sincerity Lodge (292), Anfield Lodge (2213) LC Feb 22nd 1923

Thomas Bush - Everton Lodge (823), Fairfield Lodge (2290) Dramatic Lodge (1609), Mariners Lodge (249) LDP April 21st 1920

Laurence Crosthwaite - Rock Lodge (1289) LC Jan 29th 1909

William Francis Evans - Emulation Lodge (1505) LDP May 7th 1915.

John Gunning – Hamer Lodge (1393) GLCR

John Houlding - Anfield Lodge (2213), Everton Lodge (823) and Sir Walter Raleigh Lodge (2837) LM March 18th, 1902

Simon Jude - Merchants (241), Prudence (2114), New Brighton Lodges (2619) LC Jan 2nd 1922

Thomas Knowles - Anfield Lodge (2213)

Richard L Martindale - Toxteth Lodge (1356) LC Feb 27th 1926

John McKenna - Sincerity Lodge (292), Cecil Lodge (3274) LDP March 23rd 1936

Francis Minshall - Hamer Lodge (1393), Everton Lodge (823) LC March 22nd 1902

Alexander Nisbet - Fermor Hesketh Lodge (1350), Anfield Lodge (2213). LC June 15th 1910

Fred Parry - Marlborough Lodge (1620) LC Dec 5th 1907

George Patterson – Kirkdale Lodge (1756), Anfield Lodge (2213) GLCR

John James Ramsey - Everton Lodge (823), Anfield Lodge (2213) LDP Jan 30th 1892

James Herbert Troop – Everton Lodge (823) GLCR

Tom Watson - Sincerity Lodge (292) LC May 11th 1915

Richard H. Webster - Anfield Lodge (2213) LC Oct 26th 1912

Joseph West - Merchants Lodge (241) LE Jan 3rd 1933

William Robert Williams - Hamer Lodge (1393), Sincerity Lodge (292) LDP Jan 28th 1929

Albert Worgan - Sincerity Lodge (292) LC Oct 16th 1920

Bibliography

Manuscripts and Records

Accession Box Files: Everton & Liverpool Football Clubs (Liverpool Record Office)

Cardiff, *Companies House*, Everton Football Club Company Limited, Director and Shareholder Registers, Articles and Memorandum of Association. Company File Number BT31/36624.

Cardiff, *Companies House*, Liverpool Football Club and Athletics Ground Company Limited, Director and Shareholder Registers, Articles and Memorandum of Association, Company File Number BT31/35668.

Liverpool Constitutional Association, Board Minutes and Annual Reports of County Associations, 1860-1947

Liverpool Parliamentary Debating Society Papers, 1900-1945

London, *British Newspaper Library* (Collindale), Liverpool Football Club Official Programmes

London, *Grand Lodge Library*, Grand Lodge of England Country Returns.

Works of Reference and Official Publications

Bennet R. Record of Elections, Parliamentary and Municipal: Liverpool, Birkenhead and Bootle, 1832-1900

Bolger, Paul *Edwardian A-Z and Directory of Liverpool and Bootle.* Liverpool: Stations UK, 2002

British Labour Statistics: Historical Abstract, 1886-1968. Her Majesty's Stationary Office (HMSO,1971)

Census Reports, 1841,1851, 1861, 1871, 1881, 1891, 1901

Dictionary of Edwardian Biography: Liverpool. Edinburgh: 1987

Gores Liverpool Trade Directory (Annual)

Jeremy D.J. *A Dictionary of Business Biography*, vol.3. London: Butterworth, 1985

Liverpool and Merseyside Official Red Book (Annual)

Orchard B.G. *Liverpool's Legion of Honour*. Birkenhead:1893

Newspapers and Periodicals (stored at Liverpool Record Office unless stated otherwise)

Bootle Times

Liverpool Brewers and Victuallers Journal (British Newspaper Library, Collindale, London)

Formby Times

Liverpolitan

Liverpool Athletic and Dramatic News

Liverpool Catholic Herald

Liverpool Courier

Liverpool Daily Post

Liverpool Echo

Liverpool Mercury

Liverpool Review

Porcupine

Protestant Standard

Southport Visitor

The Listener

The Xaverian

Theses and Dissertations

Brady L.W. 'T.P. O'Connor and Liverpool Politics, 1880-1929', (PhD Thesis, University of Liverpool, 1969)

Collins C.A. 'Politics and Electors in Nineteenth Century Liverpool' (MA Dissertation, University of Liverpool,1974)

Day R. 'The Motivation's of Some Football Club Director's : An Aspect of the
Social History of Association Football, 1890-1914' (MA Dissertation, University of Warwick, 1976)

Ingram P. 'Sectarianism in the North West of England: With Special Reference to Class Relationships in Liverpool, 1846-1914' (PhD Thesis, Liverpool Polytechnic, 1987)

Kennedy, D 'The Division of Everton Football Club into Hostile Factions'. PhD thesis, University of Leeds, 2003.

Klapas, J.A. 'Geographical Aspects of Religious Change in Victorian Liverpool, 1837-1901'. (Unpublished M.A. Thesis, University of Liverpool, 1977)

O'Connell, Bernard 'The Irish Nationalist Party in Liverpool, 1873-1922' (MA Dissertation, University of Liverpool, 1971)

Pooley Colin G. 'Migration, Mobility and Residential Areas in Nineteenth-Century Liverpool', (PhD Thesis, University of Liverpool, 1978)

Rees R. 'The Development of Physical Recreation in Liverpool During the Nineteenth Century (MA Dissertation, University of Liverpool, 1968)

Richardson, P.E. 'The Development of Professional Football on Merseyside, 1878-1894' (Unpublished M.A. Thesis, University of Lancaster, 1983)

Sellers I 'Liverpool Nonconformity 1786-1914' (D.Phil. Thesis, University of Keele, 1969)

Taylor Iain C. 'Black Spot on the Mersey: A Study of Environment and Society in Eighteenth and Nineteenth Century Liverpool' (PhD Thesis, University of Liverpool, 1976)

Journal Articles

Football/Sport Related:

Bairner A. and Shirlow S. 'Loyalism, Linfield and the Territorial Politics of Soccer Fandom in Northern Ireland and Sweden', *Space and Polity,* vol.2, number 2 (1998)

Bairner A. and Shirlow S. 'Territory, Politics and Soccer Fandom in Northern Ireland and Sweden', *Football Studies*, vol.3, number 1 (2000) pp.5-26

Bairner A. and Walker G. 'Football and Society in Northern Ireland: Linfield Football Club and the Case of Gerry Morgan', *Soccer and Society*, vol.2, number 1 (2001) pp.81-98

Burdsey D. and Chappell R. '"And if You Know Your History..." An Examination of the Formation of Football Clubs in Scotland and Their Role in the Construction of Socail Identity', *The Sports Historian,* number 21 (1), (2000) pp.94-106

Collins, Tony and Vamplew, Wray 'The Pub, the Drink Trade and the Early Years of Modern Football', *The Sports Historian*, 20 (2000), pp.1-17

Finn, Gerry P.T. 'Racism, Religion and Social Prejudice: Irish Catholic Clubs, Soccer and Scottish Society – I The Historical Roots of Prejudice', *International Journal of the History of Sport,* vol.8, number 1, (1991) pp.72-95

Finn, Gerry P.T. 'Racism, Religion and Social Prejudice: Irish Catholic Clubs, Soccer and Scottish Society – II Social Identities and Conspiracy Theories', *International Journal of the History of Sport* vol.8, number 3 (1991) pp.370-397

Holt, Richard 'Working Class Football and the City: The Problem of Continuity', *British Journal of Sports History,* (May 1986) pp.5-17

Kennedy, David. 'The Split of Everton Football Club, 1892: The Creation of Distinct Patterns of Boardroom Formation at Everton and Liverpool Football Club Companies', *Sport in History,* vol.23, no.1, (2003)

Kennedy, David. 'Locality and Professional Football Club Development: The Demographics of Football Club Support in Late Victorian Liverpool'.
Soccer and Society vol.5, no.3 (2004)

Kennedy, David. 'Class, Ethnicity and Civic Governance: A Social Profile of Football Club Directors on Merseyside in the Late Nineteenth Century'
International Journal of the History of Sport vol.22, no.5, (2005)

Kennedy, David. 'Community Politics in Liverpool and the Governance of Professional Football in the Late Nineteenth Century' (co-author: Professor Mike Collins, University of Leeds), *Historical Journal,* vol.49, no.3 (2006)

Kennedy, David. 'Ambiguity, Complexity and Convergence: The Evolution of Liverpool's Irish Football Clubs' (co-author: Dr Peter Kennedy), *International Journal of the History of Sport*, vol.24, no.7, (2007)

Lewis R.W. 'The Genesis of Professional Football: Bolton-Blackburn-Darwen, the Centre of Innovation, 1878-85', *The International Journal of the History of Sport*, vol.14, number 1 (1997) pp.21-54

Mason, Tony. 'The Blues and the Reds', *Transactions of the Historical Society of Lancashire and Cheshire*, Vol.134 (1985): 107-128.

General:

Bean R. 'Employers' Associations in the Port of Liverpool, 1890-1914', *International Review of Social History*, vol.21 (1976) pp.358-382

Davies, Sam 'A Stormy political Career: P.J. Kelly and Irish Nationalist and Labour Politics in Liverpool, 1891-1936', *Transactions of the Historic Society of Lancashire and Cheshire*, vol.148 (1999), pp.147-89

Jackson, Dan '"Friends of the Union": Liverpool, Ulster and Home Rule, 1910-1914', *Transactions of the Historic Society of Lancashire and Cheshire*, vol.152 (2003) pp.101-132

Munro, Alasdair 'Tramway Companies in Liverpool, 1859-1897', *Transactions of the Historic Society of Lancashire and Cheshire*, vol.119 (1967), pp.181-207

Sellers, Ian 'Nonconformist Attitudes in Later Nineteenth Century Liverpool', *Transactions of the Historic Society of Lancashire and Cheshire*, vol.114 (1963) pp.215-239

Shallice, Andy 'Orange and Green and Militancy: Sectarianism and Working Class Politics in Liverpool, 1900-1914', *Bulletin of the North West Labour History Society* number 8 (1982) pp.15-32

Smith, Joan 'Labour Tradition in Glasgow and Liverpool' *History Workshop*, 17, Spring (1984) pp.32-53

Taplin, Eric L. 'The Liverpool Trades Council, 1880-1914', *Bulletin of the North West*

Labour History Society, number 3 (1976)

Books

Armstrong G. and Giulianotti R. *Fear and Loathing in World Football*. Oxford: Berg, 2001.

Ayres, Pat. *Life and Work in Athol Street* (Liver Press, 1997)

Belchem, J. (ed). *Liverpool 800: Culture, Character and History*. Liverpool, Liverpool University Press, 2006)

Belchem, John, *Irish, Catholic and Scouse* (Liverpool University Press, 2007)

Boyle, Raymond, 'Football and Cultural Identity in Glasgow and Liverpool' (Unpublished PhD Thesis, University of Stirling, 1995)

Campbell, Tom. *Rhapsody in Green: Great Celtic Moments* (Mainstream,1990)

Clegg, Barbara. *The Man Who Made Littlewoods* (Hodder & Stoughton,1993)

Collins, Neil. *Politics and Elections in Nineteenth Century Liverpool* (Routledge, 1994)

Davies, Sam. *Liverpool Labour: Social and Political Influences on the Development of the Labour party in Liverpool, 1900-1939* (Keele, 1996)

Edge, Alan. *Faith of Our Fathers* (Mainstream, 1997)

Finn, Gerry P.T. and Guilianotti, R. (eds) *Football Culture: Local Conflicts, Global Visions* (Routledge, 2000)

Handley, James E. *The Celtic Story: A History of the Celtic Football Club* (Stanley Paul,1960)

Hickman, Mary J. *Religion, Class and Identity: The State, the Catholic Church and the Education of the Irish in Britain.* (Avebury, 1995)

Hill, David. *Out of His Skin: The John Barnes Story* (WSC Books Limited, 1989)

Kennedy, David. *A Social and Political History of Everton and Liverpool Football Clubs*
The Split, 1878-1914 (Routledge, 2016)

Kennedy, David. *Irish Football Clubs in Liverpool* (2017).

Knight, Steven. *The Brotherhood: The Secret World of Freemasonry* (HarperCollins1983)

Lugton, Alan *The Making of Hibernian,* vol.I . Edinburgh: John Donald, 1999

Mason, Tony. *The Blues and the Reds: A History of the Everton and Liverpool Football Clubs* (1985)

Murray, Bill. *The Old Firm in the New Age: Celtic and Rangers Since the Souness Revolution* (Mainstream, 1998)

Murray, Bill. *The Old Firm: Sectarianism, Sport and Society in Scotland* (revised edition. Mainstream, 2000)

Neal, Frank. *Sectarian Violence: The Liverpool Experience, 1819-1914* (Manchester University Press, 1988)

B.G. Orchard, *Liverpool Legion of Honour* (Birkenhead, 1893. Publishing House unknown)

Owen, Mike. *Everton in Europe: Der Ball ist Rund, 1962-2005* (Countyvise, 2005)

Pead, Brian *Liverpool FC, 1892-1986: A Complete Record.* Derby: Breedon Books, 1986

Redhead, Steven. *Football with Attitude* (Ashgate, 1991)

Roberts, Keith Daniel. *Liverpool Sectarianism: the Rise and Demise.* (Liverpool University Press, 2017).

Salvidge S. *Salvidge of Liverpool* (Hodder & Stoughton, 1934)

Smith T and Stuckey D. *I Did It the Hard Way* (Arthur Baker, 1980)

Sugden J. *Hosts and Champions: Soccer Cultures and National Identities.* Aldershot: Arena, 1994

Sugden J. and Bairner A. *Sport, Sectarianism and Society in a Divided Ireland.* Leicester: Leicester University Press, 1993

Waller, Phillip J. *Democracy and Sectarianism: A Political and Social History of Liverpool, 1868-1939* ((Liverpool University Press,1981)

Westcott, C. *Brian Harris: The Authorised Biography'* (NPI Media Group, 2003)

Whittingham-Jones, Barbara. *Down With the Orange Caucus* (Liverpool, 1936)

Whittingham-Jones B. *The Pedigree of Liverpool Politics. White, Orange and Green* (Liverpool, 1936)

Williams, John. *Football and Football Hooliganism in Liverpool* (Leicester University, 1987)

Williams, John (Ed) *Passing Rhythms: Liverpool FC and the Transformation of Football* (Berg, 2001)

Williams J. *Into the Red: Liverpool FC and the Changing Face of English Football* (Mainstream 2002)

Woods, J. *Growin' Up: One Scouser's Social History of Liverpool* (Palatine, 2007)

Young P.M. *Football on Merseyside* (Stanley Paul, 1963)

Notes

[1] John Williams *Into the Red: Liverpool FC and the Changing Face of English Football*, p.10.

[2] John Woods *Growin' Up: One Scouser's Social History of Liverpool*, p.43.

[3] *Liverpool Echo* (hereafter LE) 17th December 2002. 'Cilla and Ricky's "Scouseness" Test'.

[4] Tommy Smith and Dave Stuckey *I Did It the Hard Way*, p.14.

[5] See: P.Ayres, *Life and Work in Athol Street*, (Liverpool, p69; T.Campbell, *Rhapsody in Green: Great Celtic Moments*, pp.285-286; B.Clegg, *The Man Who Made Littlewoods*, p183; Alan Edge, *Faith of Our Fathers*, pp.96-99; J.E.Handley, *The Celtic Story: A History of the Celtic Football Club*, p27; D.Hill, *Out of His Skin: The John Barnes Story*, pp.68-69; B.Murray, *The Old Firm: Sectarianism, Sport and Society in Scotland*, p96n; M. Owen, *Everton in Europe: Der Ball ist Rund*, 1962-2005, p. 178-79; S. Redhead, *Football with Attitude*, p.20; T.Smith, *I Did it the Hard Way* pp.14-15; J.Williams et al, *Football and Football Hooliganism in Liverpool*, p18. See Appendix A for details.

[6] Bill Murray *The Old Firm* (2000) p.96 n19

[7] Ian Colvin, quoted in Dan Jackson, 'Friends of the Union', Liverpool, Ulster, and Home Rule, 1910-1914', *Transactions of the Historical Society of Lancashire and Cheshire*, number 152, 2003, p.114.

[8] Belchem J and MacRaild D. in: Belchem, J. (ed) 2006. P.328

[9] *Liverpool Daly Post* (Hereafter LDP) 29th October 1892.

[10] Davies, *Liverpool Labour: Social and Political Influences on the Development of the Labour party in Liverpool, 1900-1939*, p.19

[11] LDP March 30th 1892

[12] Quoted in B.G. Orchard, *Liverpool Legion of Honour*. p.490

[13] For Clayton see: Southport Liberal Association, Annual Reports, 1899-1930; Executive Committee Meeting Minutes, 1880-1930. For Baxter see: Liverpool City

Council Annual Committee and Sub-Committee Reports, 1906-1921; Baxter's funeral report, Liverpool Mercury, 28 January 1928. For Mahon see: See *Bootle Times*, 11 January and 1 March 1889 for reports of Walton Liberal Association meetings. There are no surviving records of the Liverpool Liberal Party. Confirmation of Dr Whitford's political status comes from local newspaper coverage of Liberal Party meetings during the period under review (see, for example, LDP, 13 April and 10 and 11 June 1892). Whitford's temperance credentials can be seen in *Liverpool Review* November 7th, 1896 *'Open Letter to Dr Whitford'* by 'Diogenes'. For Cuff see: press reports of local Liberal Party meetings in the early 1890s. See *Bootle Times*, 26 April 1890; LDP, 18 October 1892. For Wade (the brother of J.A.Wade, chairman of the Walton Liberal Association) see LDP, 22nd and 26th October; 1891, 5th and 11th April 1892; and 18th June. for Alfred Gates see LDP, 23rd May, 1942.

[14] Obituary notice, *LC*, 26th October, 1922 'Death of Sir W.P. Hartley', p.7; D.J.Jeremy, *Dictionary of Business Biographies*, Vol3; Jeremy, *Dictionary of Business Biographies* (1985) Hartley was vice-president of the Primitive Methodist Conference in 1892; *LC*, 7th August, 1884; See Waller, *Democracy and Sectarianism*, p.69 & p.383n. Letters from R.W. Hudson in his capacity as Kirkdale Liberal Association chairman gives his address as the soap works on Bankhall, Kirkdale, Liverpool.

[15] Liverpool Constitutional Association, minutes and annual reports, 1860-1947.

[16] Liverpool City Council Annual Committee and Sub-Committee Meeting Minutes, 1890- 1910. For H.O. Cooper details see LDP, 20 May 1915; for Thomas Croft Howarth see LDP, 13 October 1939. For Thomas McCracken see LDP, February 20, 1892 'The Tory Differences in Everton', p.5; *LDP*, February 24, 1892, 'The Late Contest in the Everton Ward', p.4. McCracken and the Liverpool FC board: 'Liverpool FC Theatrical Gala'. *Liverpool Mercury*, March 3rd 1893; 'A great day with the Liverpool Football Club'. *Liverpool Mercury*, Aug 24th 1894; 'Champagne for Mr John Houlding'. *Liverpool Mercury*, Jan 11th 1895.

[17] LDP 'Local Board Elections', p.6. April 7th, 1887

[18] 'Sir David Radcliffe disqualified'. *Bootle Times*, p.5. January 12th 1889

[19] LE December 10th, 1892

[20] LDP, 11th June 1892. See also *Porcupine*, 26 December 1896.

[21] LDP 21st Oct. 1910; Liverpool Catholic Herald 1st Nov. 1913.

[22] For Mahon see Bootle Times 8th Feb. 1890. (See also *Bootle Times*, 11th Jan.

and 1st March 1890 for more evidence of Mahon's presence with the pro Home Rule Walton Liberal Associaition.

For Baxter see: 'Loss to Liverpool Catholicity', *Liverpool Catholic Herald*, 4 Feb. 1928, 2; obituary, LDP, 28 Jan.1928). For details on Wade see LDP, June 18th 1892.

[23] *Liverpool Courier* (hereafter LC), 19th May, 1892.

[24] LDP, 29th Oct.1898; Speaking in *Porcupine*, 22nd October 1904.

[25] LDP, 17th May 1892.Waller, p.157

[26] Whittingham Jones, Barbara, The Pedigree of Liverpool Politics: White, Orange and Green, p.7. *Down With the Orange Caucus* p.6-7

[27] Salvidge of Liverpool, *Stanley Salvidge*, p.186.

[28] For details on John Houlding, Richard H.Webster, William Houlding and Thomas Croft Howarth see press reports of Working Men's Conservative Association district meetings *Bootle Times*, 4th Dec. 1886, 2 Feb. 1895; LDP, 3 Feb. 1892). For Simon Jude see LDP, 30 January 1897. For Edwin Berry see LDP, 23 Nov. 1925. For B.E. Bailey see Liverpool Conservative Association minutes and annual reports, 1890/91. For Albert E. Berry see *Liverpool and Merseyside Official Red Book*, 'Political Associations: Working Men's Conservative Association', 1925. For R.K. Milne see LDP 4th May 1953. For details for John Holland see LDP 30 Jan. 1912. For J.A. Willox see *Liverpool and Merseyside Official Red Book*, 'Political Associations: Working Men's Conservative Association' 1902. For E.P. Walker see LDP, 30th Jan. 1897 and LDP June 10th 1910. For Archibald Salvidge see Waller, *Democracy and Sectarianism* p.509. Kirkdale WMCA meeting supporting Houlding reported in LC Oct. 21st 1891; Orange Order meeting in support of Houlding reported in LDP Oct 17th 1891. For Royden, see Waller p.205. 1885 Orange Order meeting in support of Houlding and Royden: LDP July 14th 1885

[29] Finn, Gerry P.T., 'Scottish Myopias and Global Prejudices', in Finn, G.P.T. and Giullianotti, R. (eds), *Football Culture: Local Contests, Global Visions*, pp.60–1.

[30] See especially Murray B. *The Old Firm* (2000). Murray points to the various number of Celtic directors involved in Home Rule politics and the impact this had on Rangers FC, especially early in the twentieth century and the arrival in Glasgow of many Northern Irish Protestant shipyard workers bitterly opposed to Home Rule for Ireland and identified fervently with its local football rival.

[31] The significance of Freemasonry on Glasgow football culture has been touched upon by Gerry P.T. Finn, 'Racism, Religion and Social Prejudice: Irish Catholic Clubs, Soccer and Scottish Society', *International Journal of the History of Sport*, Vol.8, (1), (1991) pp.72-95, and by Bill Murray, *The Old Firm in the New Age: Celtic*

and Rangers Since the Souness Revolution, pp.173-77.

[32] LC 19 March 1902. Stephen Knight, *The Brotherhood*, p.41

[33] Liverpool FC Articles of Association, Rule 5. LDP March 30th 1892

[34] See *Athletic News* May 22nd 1899 and Aug. 14th 1899

[35] Special Resolution of Liverpool Football and Athletic Grounds Company Limited, 11th June 1906. Liverpool FC Co.File BT/35668

[36] 'Orange and Blue: St Marks (West Gorton), Arthur Connell and Manchester City Football Club'. http://www.manchesterorange.co.uk/History/st-marks-church-manchester-city-orange-order

[37] 'Masons Achieve Their Goal'. *MQ Magazine*, Issue 3 October 2002

[38] For W.C.Briggs see LC, 23 February 1923; John McKenna, LDP, 23 March 1936; JJ.Ramsey, LC, 18 October 1918. For Simon Jude, see LC, 2nd January, 1922. For A.E.Berry see LDP, 27 February 1931 Edwin Berry, LC, 23 November 1925. Hamer Lodge (1395) J.C.Brooks; Wilbraham Lodge (1713) A.E.Leyland. Source: Grand Lodge of England Country Returns.For R.L.Martindale see LC, 24th February, 1926; W.R.Williams see LDP&M, 22nd January, 1929; A.Worgan see LC, 16th October, 1920. By contrast, at Everton FC two directors of the club, John C.Brooks and Albert E.Leyland, were involved in Masonic activity in Liverpool lodges. Whilst demonstrating that no violent feeling existed against the institution of freemasonry at Everton FC, it also demonstrates that the influence of masonic activity amongst the men in control of the club was marginal. The Everton boardoom in comparison with their neighbours can be said to have been an eclectic group of men.

[39] Hickman, Mary J. *Religion, Class and Identity: The State, the Catholic Church and the Education of the Irish in Britain.*

[40] For a history of Irish Catholic attempts in Liverpool and nearby Bootle to organise independent football club representation on Merseyside see Kennedy, D. *Irish Football Clubs in Liverpool* (2017).

[41] 'I don't have fond memories of Johnny Carey', wrote Harris of his first Everton manager, 'he favoured the Irish contingent at the club and the two of us did not get on at all'. Quoted in Westcott, C., Brian Harris: *The Authorised Biography*, p.37.

[42] Young, Percy *Football on Merseyside*. p.56.

[43] 'Bravehearts of the Kop - How Scotland Made Liverpool a Bastion of Invincibility'. http://www.liverpool-kop.com/2008/03/bravehearts-of-kop-how-

scotland-made.html

[44] Figures on Liverpool's Scottish players from Liverpool FC historian Eric Doig. Eric calculates this to be 23 per cent of all playing staff at the club since its inception. Quotation regarding Liverpool's 'robust Scottish Protestantism' taken from: Hill, David *Out of His Skin: The John Barnes Story*, p.69.

[45] Williams, John (Ed), *Passing Rhythms: Liverpool FC and the Transformation of Football*, p.20)

[46] Edge, Alan. *Faith of Our Fathers*, pp.96-99

[47] Murray, Bill, *The Old Firm in the New Age: Celtic and Rangers Since the Souness Revolution*; Murray, Bill, *The Old Firm: Sectarianism, Sport and Society in Scotland*.

[48] See *The Xaverian*, January, 1899, 202-03; November, 1899, p.366. T. Mason, The Blues and the Reds: A History of the Everton and Liverpool Football Clubs, p18.

[49] Young, P. *Football on Merseyside* p.56; Belchem, John. *Irish, Catholic and Scouse*, p.242.

[50] Finn, Gerry P.T. 'Racism, Religion and Social Prejudice: Irish Catholic Clubs, Soccer and Scottish Society – II Social Identities and Conspiracy Theories', *International Journal of the History of Sport* vol.8, number 3 (1991) pp.370-397. Burdsey D. and Chappell R. '"And if You Know Your History..." *The Sports Historian*, number 21 (1), (2000) pp.94-106

[51] Boyle, Raymond, 'Football and Cultural Identity in Glasgow and Liverpool' (Unpublished PhD Thesis, University of Stirling, 1995) p.53; Mason, Tony *The Blues and the Reds: A History of the Everton and Liverpool Football Clubs*, p.17 (1985)

[52] Handley, James E. *The Celtic Story: A History of the Celtic Football Club*. Irish social and economic commentator, David McWilliams, underscores the point made by Handley in his 2007 article on the fate of what he terms 'HiBrits' (the offspring of Irish emigrants to Britain: the Hibernian- Britons). On Merseyside football, and Wayne Rooney's rise to prominence in particular, McWilliams writes that 'Father Inch [parish priest of the Blood of the Martyrs Catholic Church, Croxteth] is a Toffee true and true. Everton Football Club is the Irish team in Liverpool and it's no surprise therefore, that Rooney is a Blue.' http://www.davidmcwilliams.ie/2007/07/09/hibrits-irelands-loss-englands-gain#comments

[53] Lord Mayor Cross Liverpool Echo, 5th Jan 1932.

[54] The connection of serving club directors, secretaries and shareholders to the local Conservative Party and its affiliated organisations was still noteworthy in the Inter-War and immediate Post-War period - including leadership positions held with the avowedly sectarian Working Men's Conservative Association for directors Ralph Knowles Milne, A. E. Berry, Maxwell Fyffe. Stanley R Williams, William John Harrop, Stanley Reakes and A.B. Collins in later years would keep the club boardroom tradition of men serving as Conservative City Councillors.

Printed in Great Britain
by Amazon